simple.start
Stunning Finish

- Fabric Secrets
- Easy Piecing
- Quilting Solutions

VALORI WELLS

C&T PUBLISHING

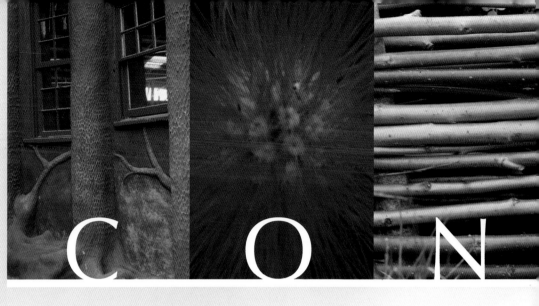

Text and Artwork copyright © 2007 by Valori Wells

Artwork copyright © 2007 by C&T Publishing, Inc.

Publisher: Amy Marson

Editorial Director: Gailen Runge

Acquisitions Editor: Jan Grigsby

Editor: Lynn Koolish

Technical Editors: Susan Nelsen and Carolyn Aune

Copyeditor/Proofreader: Wordfirm Inc.

Design Director/Cover & Book Designer: Christina D. Jarumay

Illustrator: Kirstie L. Pettersen

Production Coordinator: Zinnia Heinzmann

Quilt and how-to photography: C&T Publishing, Inc.

Inspirational photography: Valori Wells

Published by C&T Publishing, Inc., P.O. Box 1456, Lafayette, CA 94549

Library of Congress Cataloging-in-Publication Data

Wells, Valori.

Simple start–stunning finish : fabric secrets, easy piecing, quilting solutions / Valori Wells.

p. cm.

ISBN-13: 978-1-57120-378-6 (paper trade : alk. paper)

ISBN-10: 1-57120-378-8 (paper trade : alk. paper)

1. Quilting. 2. Patchwork–Patterns. 3. Applique–Patterns.
I. Title.

TT835.W47849 2007

746.46'041–dc22

2007000416

Printed in China

10 9 8 7 6 5 4 3 2 1

C O N

T E N T S

CURVE PIECING/ CIRCLE APPLIQUÉ

PAPER-PIECING

FOREWORD

Watching a quilter grow, creating new ideas and inspiring others, is a real treat. When the quilter is your own daughter, who you never thought would sew, it is even more special. Since Valori joined The Stitchin' Post nine years ago, I have seen her work through many a traditional quilt pattern, always making it her own. I think that her art school background, her experience in fabric design, and her work with quilters and knitters have made her an enlightened quilt designer.

Because she is involved in more than one aspect of the business, she is more knowledgeable about what customers want to make and what fabrics they like. She also works in her studio designing quilts and fabric five days a week in the afternoons. What a treat it is to visit and see a large canvas on the easel being painted with a yellow-gold sunflower, a stack of fabric for the next quilt, a quilt being designed on the wall, a drawing on the drawing board for the next line of fabric, a quilt being quilted at the sewing machine, and stacks of photos on the table, along with photos of her husband, daughter, and pets on the bulletin board. Everywhere you look, something creative is happening. This is what makes Valori the successful designer she is. As we say, she will never run out of things to do creatively.

Her sense of color is intuitive. She just knows how to balance values and color families when designing quilts and fabrics. It takes my breath away watching her make these decisions. Being invited over so she can run things by me is a treat. She already knows what to do, but verbalizing it to Mom seems to work. Once in a while, I do have a valid opinion.

You are in for a treat with *Simple Start—Stunning Finish.* What started out as simple circle designs led to rectangles and simple curve piecing. The quilts are easy and attainable, yet interesting, and they offer many possibilities for design as well as inspiring fabric and color ideas. Don't forget to look at the quilting designs on Valori's quilts. They too are very innovative and appealing. Pick your piecing technique, select your fabric, and finish your stunning quilt with an inspired quilting design.

JEAN WELLS KEENAN

PREFACE

Prints (especially large-scale prints), solid fabrics, simple designs, and inspired quilting are the essence of this book. As I explore quiltmaking I find myself drawn to simpler shapes, allowing the fabric or the quilting design to create the visual complexity.

In the creative process of quiltmaking and fabric design, I find that I am constantly gaining inspiration from the world around me. My stepping-stone for design and color is my photography. The lens of the camera frames what I see; it creates a structural image, which can lead to quilts, quilting lines, and fabric designs. I've included some of my sources of inspiration to give you some ideas.

I am drawn to large-scale prints. I design them, I purchase them, and I use them in quilts. Planning designs to feature large-scale prints is a challenge I really enjoy. The large-scale print can make a simple quilt design look complex.

As much as I love large-scale prints, my other passion is for solid and solid-like fabrics. Hand-dyed and solid fabrics show off quilting lines and allow me to express design in another way. Solid colors also make it possible to make subtle color changes within a quilt, especially when quilting. In some of my quilts I draw on both solids and large-scale prints to communicate my ideas.

With this book I hope to give you some new ideas and inspire you to find passion in your quilting world. The simple quilt designs in this book are achievable as well as beautiful, and in using them you'll have a chance to explore color, value, fabric choice, and quilting lines. In this day and age, time is precious, yet creating something by hand as a gift or for yourself is very rewarding, which is why simple designs like these fit into today's lifestyle.

VALORI

INTRODUCTION

FABRIC SECRETS

LARGE-SCALE PRINTS

Large-scale prints provide so much inspiration! Become a detective, and isolate the color families that you see in them. Look for the color family that is used the most and the one that is used the least. Use this information to choose the theme color and an accent color for your quilt. When you use a large piece of a large-scale print, it not only becomes the color theme but it determines the style of the quilt as well. As a bonus, when you cut up a large-scale print, you get multiple color and texture stories because of the variety of colors and shapes that result.

SOLID AND SOLID-LIKE FABRICS

Solid and solid-like (hand-dyes, mottled, tone-on-tone) fabrics can stand alone in a quilt or support a printed fabric. Using these fabrics alone can be a great way to showcase your quilting design. Another wonderful use for these fabrics is for the quilt back. When quilted, the stitched design will create another story on the back, making a two-sided quilt.

② EASY PIECING AND APPLIQUÉ

STRAIGHT PIECING

A simple way to get started on a quilt is to use strips and rectangles of fabric. One of the classic piecing designs from the past is simple strip piecing. Even better, when you put rectangles into a pattern like *Retro Romance* (page 17), you get a wonderful secondary design. Take this same concept and turn a rectangle into a wedge shape to create angles and interest in a design. Use any of these simple techniques to create stunning designs.

SIMPLE CURVE PIECING

Add a simple curve to a straight line, and you get movement and contrast in a quilt design. Gentle curves are easy to piece and can resemble features in a landscape.

PAPER-FOUNDATION PIECING

Paper-foundation piecing is perfect for stitching precise points and strong lines. Create dynamic designs with this technique.

BLIND-HEM-STITCH APPLIQUÉ

With blind-hem-stitch appliqué, circles have never been easier. This machine technique is foolproof, even for the beginner.

RAW-EDGE APPLIQUÉ

If you're a free spirit who wants a more textured look and the quick satisfaction of appliqué, try the raw-edge technique.

③ QUILTING SOLUTIONS

ECHO QUILTING

Echo quilting is the easiest of the quilting techniques. Take elements from the fabric or piecing to use as the quilting lines, and change the size or color of the elements. This repetitive approach creates continuity within the quilt.

SKETCH QUILTING

Use sketch quilting to create a design that resembles a sketch or a simple line drawing on the top of the quilt surface. This free-motion quilting technique works best for an overall design, such as the tree used in *The Red Tree* (page 49). Be sure to use many different colors of thread stitched over each other, as you would when sketching with colored pencils.

PLAYFUL QUILTING

Playful quilting interacts with the fabric to create a secondary pattern on the quilt top. *Circle Around* (page 56) is a perfect example of this quilting style. Notice how the quilted circles on the solid fabric create playful lines.

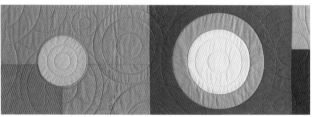

FLUID QUILTING

When there is a lot of activity in the fabric or quilt design, the quilting should be a subtle accent on the entire surface so that it enhances the overall design rather than competing with it. For example, on *Effervescence* (page 61) the quilting is a simple swirl shape that relates to the circles and supports the concept but doesn't compete with them.

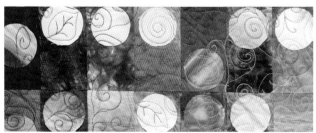

FLORAL SORBET

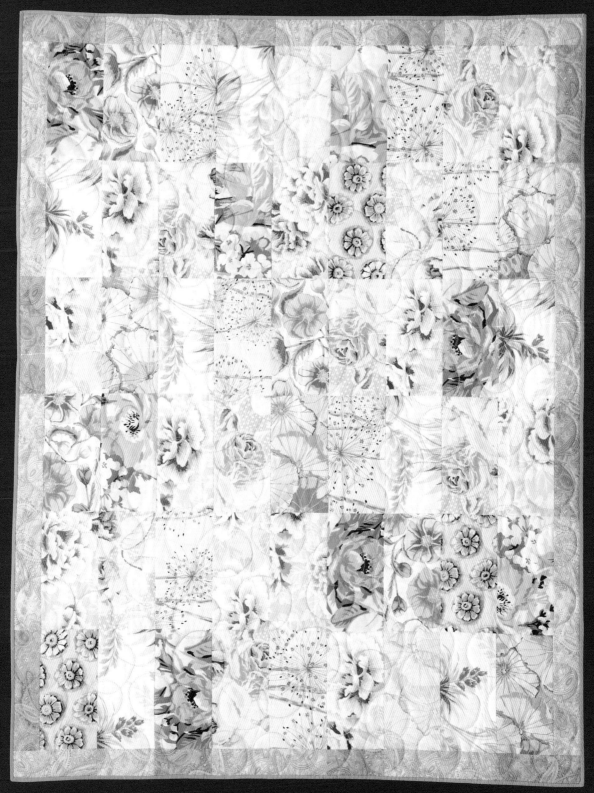

Finished size: 49˝ × 64˝

1 FABRIC: Large-scale prints

2 PIECING: Straight (rectangles)

3 QUILTING: Playful

This design works well with any family of large-scale prints, not just florals—take a look at page 11 for tips on selecting your family of large-scale prints. *Floral Sorbet* was created for my daughter. It seemed perfect with the large-scale prints and the playfulness of the quilted circles.

After *Effervescence* (page 61) was completed, I wanted to make a larger-scale version. I was pregnant when I started this quilt, and I was pretty sure we were having a little girl—so I decided that this quilt would be for her. I planned to use large-scale prints and then appliqué circles on the rectangles, as I did for *Effervescence*. I selected a variety of large-scale prints in the same color family and mood, but once the prints were on the wall I realized that the circles would take away from the beauty of the large-scale prints. One of the benefits of using large-scale prints is that when you cut them up, you get different elements of the fabric design with each cut. It is an easy way to get complexity while keeping your overall design simple. I decided that quilting the circles would provide the circular element I was looking for, along with the contrast to the straight lines of the block, without taking away from the beauty of the fabrics.

MATERIALS

- 2¾ yards total or ¼ yard each of 14 different large-scale prints for blocks
- ⅝ yard total or ¼ yard each of 3 different paisleys for borders
- 3 yards for backing
- ½ yard for binding
- 53″ × 68″ batting

CUTTING

Large-scale prints:

Cut 54 rectangles 5½″ × 10½″ for the blocks.

Paisleys:

Cut 12 rectangles 2½″ × 10½″ for the side borders.

Cut 14 rectangles 2½″ × 5½″ for the top and bottom borders.

Cut 4 rectangles 2½″ × 7½″ for the border corners.

ASSEMBLY

BLOCKS

1. After you have cut out all the pieces, arrange the large-scale print rectangles on a design wall or the floor. Place them 9 across and 6 down.

2. Stitch the rectangles together in rows. Start at the top, and work down. Press the seam allowances in alternate directions for each row so the seams nest when you sew the rows together.

3. Stitch the rows together, and press.

BORDERS

1. Refer to the Quilt Assembly Diagram to lay out the borders, using the paisley rectangles around the quilt center. Make sure the seams of the rectangles line up with the seams of the blocks.

2. Stitch the rectangles together for the top, bottom, and side borders. Press the seams so they nest with the quilt center seams.

3. Stitch the side borders to the quilt center and press.

4. Stitch the top and bottom borders to the quilt and press.

FINISHING

1. Layer the backing, batting, and quilt top. Baste, and quilt as desired.

2. Bind using your preferred method.

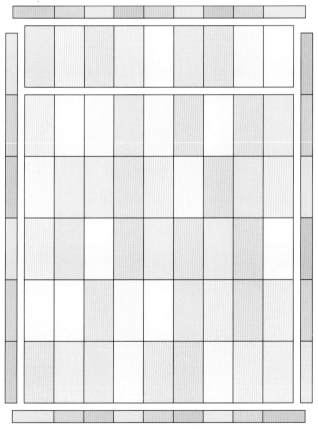

Quilt Assembly Diagram

PLAYFUL QUILTING

Quilting a perfect circle is tough, and there are times when the perfection of an exact circle is what you want. A great way to create circles is to go over the initial quilting lines three or more times so that you don't see that they are imperfect. It makes the quilt seem more sketchy, loose, and free-form. This effect really comes out after washing, when the quilt shrinks a bit. For a real vintage "shrink effect," and for warmth, use wool batting.

Although this quilt does not have any circles on the fabric, the circle design creates a playful secondary pattern without distracting from the fabrics. Quilt overlapping circles free-form, using multiple layers. Select a thread color that is similar to that of the quilt so that it blends with the fabric but allows you to see the impressions of the circles.

tips & techniques

Choosing Large-Scale Prints

To make your quilt successful, you should remember a few things when choosing large-scale prints.

1. Choose a color theme. Find some prints that keep the mood but aren't necessarily the same colors as the main palette. *Floral Sorbet* uses predominately a soft pink palette, but prints with other colors add variety while keeping the mood.

2. Choose some prints that are compact.

3. Choose some prints with airy designs that have more background.

4. Choose some prints that are monochromatic. Subtle prints give the eye a place to rest.

5. Choose some prints that have multiple colors. When prints with lots of colors are cut up, some pieces will read one color, and some pieces will read a different color.

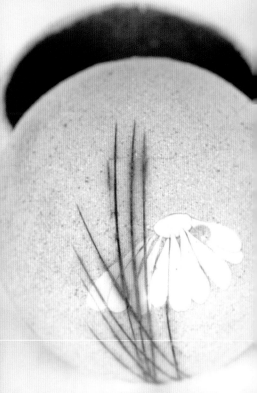

VINTAGE FLORAL

Quilted by Lori Gailey. Finished size: 60¾" × 79"

1 **FABRIC:** Large-scale prints and solids

2 **PIECING:** Straight and strip piecing

3 **QUILTING:** Echo

Vintage Floral is true to its name, with the pretty rose floral coupled with antique-looking small prints for the sashing. A Japanese floral print provided the initial inspiration for this quilt.

Mosaics have always been fascinating to me, and the print gave me all the cues I needed to choose the fabrics used in the mosaic-like sashing. To piece the sashing, I broke the design down into its smallest parts, then figured out how to strip piece them. (Quilters always find ways of creating detail with piecing.) See page 16 for an easy way to make these complex-looking strips.

To make the sashing colors appear as little jewels, I used the neutral beiges for the larger rectangles, and the deeper reds and greens for the smaller squares and rectangles. Notice how all the beiges are different shades. The slight differences in value make the mosaic piecing more interesting and catch the eye here and there.

Let your favorite vintage fabrics bloom into your *Vintage Floral*.

MATERIALS

- 1½ yards large-scale theme print for block centers
- 2¾ yards total light prints/neutral beiges for sashing and corner posts
- 1¼ yards total dark prints for sashing and corner posts
- 2⅝ yards solid for background and binding
- 3⅝ yards for backing
- 65″ × 83″ batting

CUTTING

Large-scale theme print:

Cut 5 strips 9½″ × 42″. From these cut 18 squares 9½″ × 9½″ for the blocks.

Solid background:

Cut 3 squares 20½″ × 20½″. Cut each diagonally twice for the setting triangles.

Cut diagonally twice.

Cut 2 squares 13½″ × 13½″. Cut diagonally once for the corners.

Cut diagonally once.

Light prints/neutral beiges:

Cut 10 strips 4½″ × 42″ for the sashing and corner posts.

Cut 14 strips 2½″ × 42″ for the sashing and corner posts.

Dark prints:

Cut 12 strips 1½″ × 42″ for the sashing and corner posts.

Cut 20 strips 1″ × 42″ for the sashing and corner posts.

ASSEMBLY

MAKE THE SASHING AND CORNER POSTS

1. The sashing and corner posts are made from a variety of pieced strip sets. To make the strip sets, follow the illustration below to arrange the light and dark strips in each of the 3 combinations shown. The cut strip widths are given for each combination. You will need 10 total sets of strips. None of the strip sets have to be alike, so fabrics can change position. The strip sets need to measure 9½″ wide when sewn together. Because there are so many seams in each set, it is important for you to use an accurate ¼″ seam allowance, and press the seam allowances in one direction. After the first strip set is stitched together, measure it to see if it is 9½″ wide. If it is too narrow, your seam allowance was too large and needs to be adjusted. If the set is too large, trim it to 9½″ wide. Remember that being off a couple of threads in several seams can add up quickly.

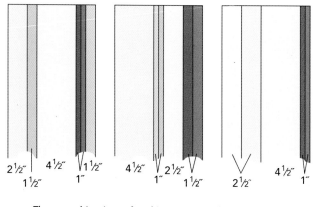

Three combinations of sashing strip sets (measurements are cut widths)

2. Once all the strip sets are complete and pressed, cut them into 1½″ sections as shown.

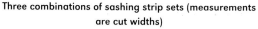
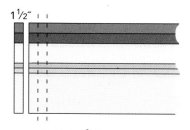

Cut into 1½″ sections.

3. Randomly arrange the sections from the strip sets into groups of 4 as shown. Stitch the strip sets together, and press. Make 64 units. Set aside 48 of these units for sashing.

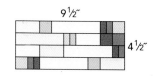

Arrange 1½″ sections into groups of 4 for sashing.

4. Cut the remaining 16 units from Step 3 into 4½″ × 4½″ squares for corner posts as shown.

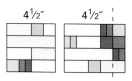

Cut 31 corner posts.

PUT THE BLOCKS TOGETHER

1. Refer to the Quilt Assembly Diagram (page 16) to lay out the blocks, sashing, and corner posts. Add the setting triangles and corner triangles to the layout. All the triangles are oversized and will be trimmed later. Stitch only the blocks, sashing, and corner posts together diagonally row by row, following the row numbers. Press all the seams toward the blocks and away from the corner posts. Do not join the rows yet.

2. Now join Rows 1 and 2 together, and press. Then add Setting Triangles A and B as shown. Press the seams toward the triangles. Stitch Rows 3 and 4, and add Setting Triangles C and D. Press. Continue joining rows and the setting triangles in sequence.

3. Join the row sections together. Add the 4 corner triangles last. Press.

4. Use a rotary cutter and a see-through ruler to trim the setting triangles and corners to ¼" beyond the point of the corner posts.

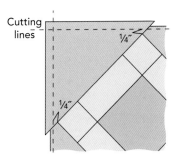

Trim setting triangles and corners.

FINISHING

1. Layer the backing, batting, and quilt top. Baste, and quilt as desired.

2. Bind using your preferred method.

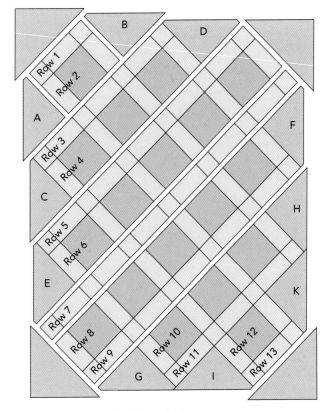

Quilt Assembly Diagram

ECHO QUILTING

The vintage fabric dictated the quilting for *Vintage Floral* because I wanted to keep the feel of the quilting consistent with the antique feel of the fabric. The flowers and leaves of the large floral print are outlined and echoed by the quilting. A fern pattern from the print carries the same feeling into the sashing, setting triangles, and corners.

tips & techniques

Adding Strip-Pieced Details

Complex-looking details can add richness to an otherwise simple quilt. Here's how to make the simple piecing look complex.

1. Use different widths of fabric for a more interesting look.

2. Piece smaller widths of darker fabrics into a lighter background.

3. Stitch the strips together into different configurations.

4. Cut the strips into random lengths, and piece together.

5. Use in multiple rows to multiply the effect.

RETRO ROMANCE

Finished size: 45˝ × 70˝

1 **FABRIC:** Theme prints and solids

2 **PIECING:** Straight (Courthouse Steps)

3 **QUILTING:** Echo

A great way to begin a quilt is to use your favorite theme print as a starting point. I love the theme print in *Retro Romance*, especially its complexity; I wasn't sure what I was going to make with it, but I knew something would come out of it.

Courthouse Steps is one of my favorite blocks, especially when just one color is used to go around the center. I started sketching out different sizes of blocks that would work together in a square (25″ × 25″) and eventually came up with this design. I realized that the whole quilt needed to be bigger to make more of a statement, but I liked the way the blocks were arranged. To solve the dilemma I made another set of blocks, just like the first set. I rearranged the blocks but kept coming back to the original plan. Once again, my mantra of keeping it simple provided the best design solution.

To make your own *Retro Romance,* start with the theme print as your inspiration. Then select solid colors that relate to the theme; to start, pick as many colors as you want. Now, simplify the palette by eliminating colors: select the color for the centers of the blocks, then pick five colors to go with that center color. As you select your solids, you'll realize that you won't find perfect matches to your theme print, so go with similar shades and it will work. On page 21 you will find tips to help you select just the right companion colors.

MATERIALS

- ⅜ yard salmon solid for blocks

- ⅜ yard pink solid for blocks

- ⅜ yard gold solid for blocks

- ⅓ yard orange solid for blocks

- ¼ yard green solid for blocks

- ⅞ yard brown solid for block centers and narrow insert

- 1¾ yards large-scale theme print for borders

- 2¾ yards for backing

- ½ yard for binding

- 49″ × 74″ batting

CUTTING

Refer to the Section Diagram on page 20.

Block A

Brown: Cut 2 rectangles 3″ × 8½″ for the block centers.

Salmon solid:

Cut 2 rectangles 2½″ × 10½″ for A4.

Cut 2 rectangles 2″ × 10½″ for A3.

Cut 4 rectangles 1½″ × 3″ for A1 and A2.

Block B

Brown: Cut 2 squares 3½″ × 3½″ for the block centers.

Green solid:

Cut 4 rectangles 2″ × 6½″ for B3 and B4.

Cut 4 rectangles 2″ × 3½″ for B1 and B2.

Block C

Brown: Cut 2 rectangles 3″ × 6½″ for the block centers.

Gold solid:

Cut 2 rectangles 2½″ × 9½″ for C3.

Cut 2 rectangles 2″ × 9½″ for C4.

Cut 4 rectangles 2″ × 3″ for C1 and C2.

Block D

Brown: Cut 2 rectangles 2½″ × 4½″ for the block centers.

Green solid:

Cut 4 rectangles 1½″ × 6½″ for D3 and D4.

Cut 4 rectangles 1½″ × 2½″ for D1 and D2.

Block E

Brown: Cut 2 rectangles 2½″ × 5½″ for the block centers.

Gold solid:

Cut 2 rectangles 3″ × 8½″ for E4.

Cut 2 rectangles 2″ × 8½″ for E3.

Cut 4 rectangles 2″ × 2½″ for E1 and E2.

Block F

Brown: Cut 2 rectangles 3½″ × 4½″ for the block centers.

Pink solid:

Cut 4 rectangles 2″ × 7½″ for F3 and F4.

Cut 4 rectangles 2″ × 3½″ for F1 and F2.

Block G

Brown: Cut 2 rectangles 4″ × 4½″ for the block centers.

Pink solid:

Cut 2 rectangles 2½″ × 7½″ for G3.

Cut 2 rectangles 2″ × 7½″ for G4.

Cut 4 rectangles 2″ × 4″ for G1 and G2.

Block H

Brown: Cut 2 squares 4½″ × 4½″ for the block centers.

Salmon solid:

Cut 4 rectangles 2″ × 7½″ for H3 and H4.

Cut 4 rectangles 2″ × 4½″ for H1 and H2.

Block I

Brown: Cut 2 rectangles 2½″ × 5½″ for the block centers.

Green solid:

Cut 4 rectangles 2″ × 7½″ for I3 and I4.

Cut 4 rectangles 1½″ × 2½″ for I1 and I2.

Block J

Brown: Cut 2 rectangles 2½″ × 5½″ for the block centers.

Orange solid:

Cut 4 rectangles 2½″ × 9½″ for J3 and J4.

Cut 4 squares 2½″ × 2½″ for J1 and J2.

Block K

Brown: Cut 2 rectangles 3″ × 7½″ for the block centers.

Gold solid:

Cut 2 rectangles 2½″ × 10½″ for K3.

Cut 2 rectangles 2″ × 10½″ for K4.

Cut 4 rectangles 2″ × 3″ for K1 and K2.

Block L

Brown: Cut 2 rectangles 3½″ × 4½″ for the block centers.

Orange solid:

Cut 4 rectangles 1½″ × 6½″ for L3 and L4.

Cut 4 rectangles 1½″ × 3½″ for L1 and L2.

Block M

Brown: Cut 2 rectangles 2½″ × 3½″ for the block centers.

Pink solid:

Cut 4 rectangles 2″ × 6½″ for M3 and M4.

Cut 4 rectangles 2″ × 2½″ for M1 and M2.

Block N

Brown: Cut 2 rectangles 3″ × 6½″ for the block centers.

Salmon solid:

Cut 2 rectangles 2½″ × 9½″ for N3.

Cut 2 rectangles 2″ × 9½″ for N4.

Cut 2 rectangles 2½″ × 3″ for N2.

Cut 2 rectangles 1½″ × 3″ for N1.

Brown:

Cut 4 strips ¾″ × 42″ for the narrow insert. Stitch the strips together. From the long strip:

Cut 2 strips ¾″ × 50½″.

Cut 2 strips ¾″ × 25½″.

Large-scale theme print:

Cut 5 strips 10½″ × 42″ for the border. Stitch the strips together. From the long strip:

Cut 2 strips 10½″ × 70½″.

Cut 2 strips 10½″ × 25½″.

ASSEMBLY

MAKE THE BLOCKS

Refer to the Section Diagram to construct the blocks. Stitch Pieces 1 and 2 to the block center first, and press to the center. Then add Pieces 3 and 4, and press. Complete 2 of each block.

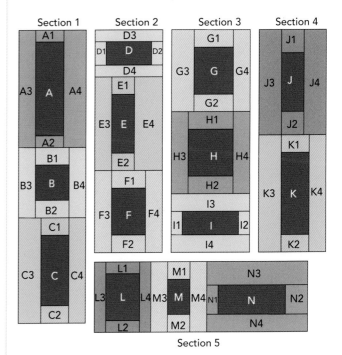

Section Diagram

PUT THE BLOCKS TOGETHER

1. Arrange the blocks on a design wall or the floor, referring again to the Section Diagram.

2. Stitch Blocks A, B, and C together to make Section 1. Press. Stitch Sections 2, 3, 4, and 5, and press each section.

3. Join Sections 2, 3, and 4 together. Press. Add Section 5 to the bottom of 2 3 4, and add Section 1 to complete the top half of the quilt center.

4. Repeat Steps 1–3 to complete the bottom half. Refer to the Quilt Assembly Diagram, and join the top and bottom sections. Press.

BORDERS

1. Press the brown insert strips in half, wrong sides together, and pin a strip onto each side of the quilt, overlapping at the corners.

2. Stitch the top and bottom borders to the quilt top. Press.

3. Stitch the side borders to the quilt top. Press.

FINISHING

1. Layer the backing, batting, and quilt top. Baste, and quilt as desired or use the quilting suggestion below.

2. Bind using your preferred method.

Quilt Assembly Diagram

ECHO QUILTING

Keep it simple when quilting. Take your cues from the theme print, and outline the large areas in the print. This is also a great way to gain confidence while learning to free-motion quilt. Use straight-line quilting with a walking foot for the Courthouse Steps blocks. This ensures that the quilting complements and accents the design.

tips & techniques

Choosing Companion Colors

Here's how to use a theme print to choose your companion colors.

1. Start by selecting fabrics that have colors similar to those in your theme print. It is usually hard to find exact color matches, but something close is just fine.

2. Decide which color in the theme print you like most, and use that color as the dominant color in your quilt. In *Retro Romance*, I selected brown as the dominant solid, and the final design really emphasized the dark brown in the theme print.

3. Lay out the fabrics in proportion to how much of each will be used in the quilt. One way is to stack all the fabrics so only small amounts of the color show, except for your selected dominant color, which should show more. Then place the theme print across your stacks.

4. Step back so you can see how the fabrics interact. If you aren't sure you like what you see, try using another color as the dominant color.

DAISY MAE

Finished size: 42″ × 72″

PAINTED GRASS

Finished size: 24˝ × 56˝

1 **FABRIC:** Solids

2 **PIECING:** Straight (creating wedges out of rectangles)

3 **QUILTING:** Fluid

The initial inspiration for *Painted Grass* came from a photo of a rug I saw in a home magazine. I was enjoying a cup of coffee at my girlfriend Sarah's new café and saw a photograph of a hallway with a great rug. My initial thought was that it would make an interesting quilt. Several weeks later, I thought about that rug. I do not have a photographic memory, so I used what I thought I remembered about the rug—the proportion of the length to the width and the different sizes of rectangles that were put together to create the length in the design. I made the idea my own by using different sizes of strips and wedges to create the rectangles.

The rich combination of reds, pinks, oranges, and yellows is one of my favorites. An important design decision in this type of quilt is how much of each color to use. You need to decide which colors are your key colors and which colors are your accent colors—if you use the same amount of each color, the quilt won't be very interesting. When working with solids, you must also focus on the values of the colors. In Tips and Techniques on page 34, read more about the importance of value when using solids.

Find ideas from your surroundings as I did for *Painted Grass*, and make them unique by changing sizes or adding or subtracting detail.

MATERIALS

Painted Grass showcases 17 different solid-colored fabrics. You may not be able to find 17 fabrics that you like, so you can double up on some. Refer to the photograph of the quilt to plan your palette. Make sure you have lights and brights as well as darks in order to have contrast and interest in this solid-colored quilt.

- 3⅛ yards total of 17 different solids (¼ yard each of 8 different solids and ⅛ yard each of 9 different solids) for blocks
- 1⅔ yards for backing
- ⅜ yard for binding
- 28″ × 60″ batting

CUTTING AND SEWING

This quilt is made of angled wedges and rectangles. The illustrations show how to cut the wedges. I recommend cutting out the entire row of wedges and strips, and then arranging them on a design wall before sewing them together. Refer to the Quilt Assembly Diagram on page 33.

SPECIAL CUTTING AND LABELING NOTE: Always place fabrics right side up when layering and cutting. Part of each rectangle will be discarded or can be used for another project. Follow the schematic, and place the ruler on the line indicated as the cutting line. Then pull apart the wedges, and place the "keeper" wedges together as shown. Label the pieces in each step.

ROW F CUTTING AND CONSTRUCTION

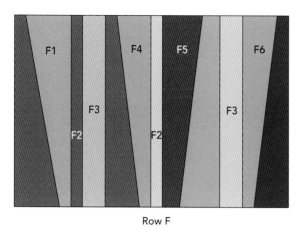

Row F

Begin with Row F because these large rectangles need to be cut on the crosswise grain using the ¼-yard cuts of fabric.

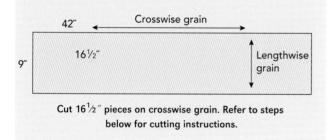

Cut 16½" pieces on crosswise grain. Refer to steps below for cutting instructions.

1. F1: Layer 2 fabrics right sides up, and cut a rectangle 4½" × 16½". Line up the ruler 1½" from the top left edge, angling to the bottom right corner. Cut as shown. Discard the B wedges. Combine 2 A wedges to make 1 rectangle.

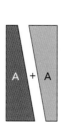

Cut wedges for F1. Sew A wedges together.

2. F2: Layer 2 fabrics right sides up, and cut a rectangle 1½" × 16½".

3. F3: Layer 2 fabrics right sides up, and cut a rectangle 2½" × 16½".

4. F4: Layer 2 fabrics right sides up, and cut a rectangle 3½" × 16½". Cut as shown. Discard the B wedges. Combine 2 A wedges to make 1 rectangle.

Cut wedges for F4. Sew A wedges together.

5. F5: Layer 2 fabrics right sides up, and cut a rectangle 4" × 16½". Cut as shown. Discard the A wedges. Combine 2 B wedges to make 1 rectangle.

Cut wedges for F5. Sew B wedges together.

6. F6: Layer 2 fabrics right sides up, and cut a rectangle 3½" × 16½". Cut as shown. Discard the A wedges. Combine 2 B wedges to make 1 rectangle.

Cut wedges for F6. Sew B wedges together.

7. Refer to the Quilt Assembly Diagram, and arrange the pieces as indicated for Row F. Stitch the wedges and rectangles together. Press each seam. Set aside.

ROW E CUTTING AND CONSTRUCTION

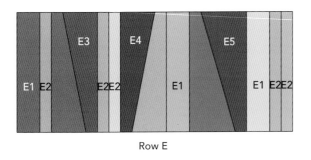

Row E

1. E1: Layer 3 fabrics right sides up, and cut a rectangle 2½″ × 10½″.

2. E2: Layer 5 fabrics right sides up, and cut a rectangle 1½″ × 10½″.

3. E3: Layer 2 fabrics right sides up, and cut a rectangle 3½″ × 10½″. Cut as shown. Discard the B wedges. Combine 2 A wedges to make 1 rectangle.

Cut wedges for E3. Sew A wedges together.

4. E4: Layer 2 fabrics right sides up, and cut a rectangle 3½″ × 10½″. Cut as shown. Discard the A wedges. Combine 2 B wedges to make 1 rectangle.

Cut wedges for E4. Sew B wedges together.

5. E5: Layer 2 fabrics right sides up, and cut a rectangle 4½″ × 10½″. Cut as shown. Discard the B wedges. Combine 2 A wedges to make 1 rectangle.

Cut wedges for E5. Sew A wedges together.

6. Refer to the Quilt Assembly Diagram, and arrange the pieces as indicated for Row E. Stitch the wedges and rectangles together. Press each seam. Set aside.

ROW D CUTTING AND CONSTRUCTION

Row D

1. D1: Layer 4 fabrics right sides up, and cut a rectangle 3½″ × 6½″. Cut as shown. Discard the B wedges. Combine the A wedges to make 2 rectangles.

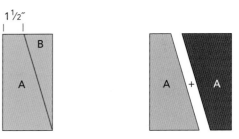

Cut wedges for D1. Sew A wedges together.

2. D2: Layer 3 fabrics right sides up, and cut a rectangle 1½″ × 6½″.

3. D3: Layer 2 fabrics right sides up, and cut a rectangle 2½″ × 6½″.

4. D4: Layer 2 fabrics right sides up, and cut a rectangle 4″ × 6½″. Cut as shown. Discard the A wedges. Combine 2 B wedges to make 1 rectangle.

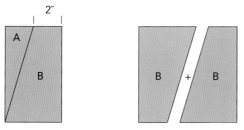

Cut wedges for D4. Sew B wedges together.

5. D5: Layer 2 fabrics right sides up, and cut a rectangle 3½″ × 6½″. Cut as shown. Discard the A wedges. Combine 2 B wedges to make 1 rectangle.

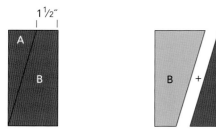

Cut wedges for D5. Sew B wedges together.

6. Refer to the Quilt Assembly Diagram, and arrange the pieces as indicated for Row D. Stitch the wedges and rectangles together. Press each seam. Set aside.

ROW C CUTTING AND CONSTRUCTION

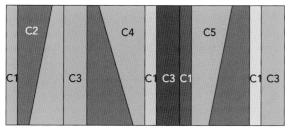

Row C

1. C1: Layer 4 fabrics right sides up, and cut a rectangle 1½″ × 10½″.

2. C2: Layer 2 fabrics right sides up, and cut a rectangle 3½″ × 10½″. Cut as shown. Discard the A wedges. Combine 2 B wedges to make 1 rectangle.

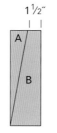
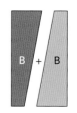

Cut wedges for C2. Sew B wedges together.

3. C3: Layer 3 fabrics right sides up, and cut a rectangle 2½″ × 10½″.

4. C4: Layer 2 fabrics right sides up, and cut a rectangle 4½″ × 10½″. Cut as shown. Discard the A wedges. Combine 2 B wedges to make 1 rectangle.

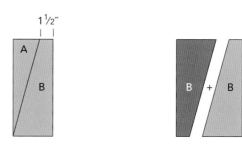

Cut wedges for C4. Sew B wedges together.

5. C5: Layer 2 fabrics right sides up, and cut a rectangle 4″ × 10½″. Cut as shown. Discard the A wedges. Combine 2 B wedges to make 1 rectangle.

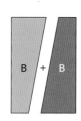

Cut wedges for C5. Sew B wedges together.

6. Refer to the Quilt Assembly Diagram, and arrange the pieces as indicated for Row C. Stitch the wedges and rectangles together. Press each seam. Set aside.

ROW B CUTTING AND CONSTRUCTION

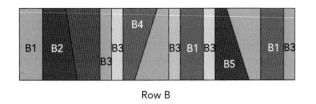

Row B

1. B1: Layer 3 fabrics right sides up, and cut a rectangle 2½" × 6½".

2. B2: Layer 2 fabrics right sides up, and cut a rectangle 3½" × 6½". Cut as shown. Discard the B wedges. Combine 2 A wedges to make 1 rectangle.

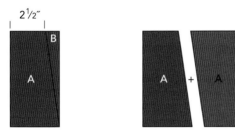

Cut wedges for B2. Sew A wedges together.

3. B3: Layer 5 fabrics right sides up, and cut a rectangle 1½" × 6½".

4. B4: Layer 2 fabrics right sides up, and cut a rectangle 3½" × 6½". Cut as shown. Discard the A wedges. Combine 2 B wedges to make 1 rectangle.

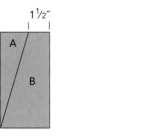

Cut wedges for B4. Sew B wedges together.

5. B5: Layer 2 fabrics right sides up, and cut a rectangle 3½" × 6½". Cut as shown. Discard the B wedges. Combine 2 A wedges to make 1 rectangle.

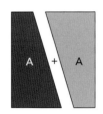

Cut wedges for B5. Sew A wedges together.

6. Refer to the Quilt Assembly Diagram, and arrange the pieces as indicated for Row B. Stitch the wedges and rectangles together. Press each seam. Set aside.

ROW A CUTTING AND CONSTRUCTION

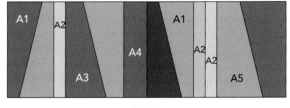

Row A

1. A1: Layer 4 fabrics right sides up, and cut a rectangle 3½" × 8½". Cut as shown. Discard the A wedges. Combine the B wedges to make 2 rectangles.

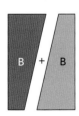

Cut wedges for A1. Sew B wedges together.

2. A2: Layer 3 fabrics right sides up, and cut a rectangle 1½″ × 8½″.

3. A3: Layer 2 fabrics right sides up, and cut a rectangle 4″ × 8½″. Cut as shown. Discard the B wedges. Combine 2 A wedges to make 1 rectangle.

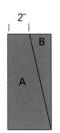

Cut wedges for A3. Sew A wedges together.

4. A4: From 1 layer of fabric, cut a rectangle 2½″ × 8½″.

5. A5: Layer 2 fabrics right sides up, and cut a rectangle 4½″ × 8½″. Cut as shown. Discard the B wedges. Combine 2 A wedges to make 1 rectangle.

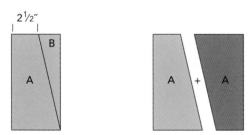

Cut wedges for A5. Sew A wedges together.

6. Refer to the Quilt Assembly Diagram, and arrange the pieces as indicated for Row A. Stitch the wedges and rectangles together. Press each seam. Set aside.

ASSEMBLY

Refer to the Quilt Assembly Diagram to arrange the rows. Stitch the rows together. Press.

FINISHING

1. Layer the backing, batting, and quilt top. Baste, and quilt as desired or use the quilting suggestion below.

2. Bind using your preferred method.

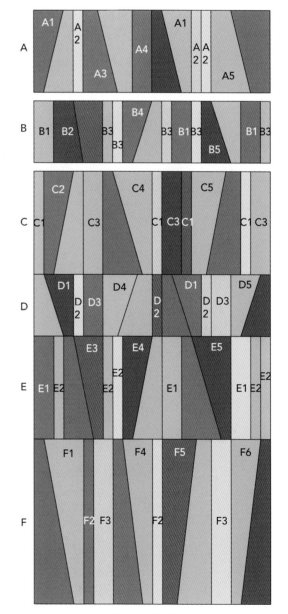

Quilt Assembly Diagram

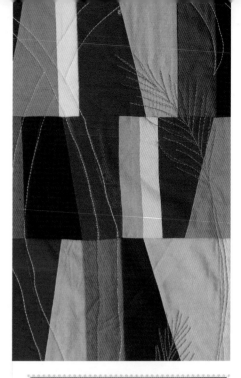

FLUID QUILTING

For *Painted Grass* I chose to quilt a single layer of simple, fluid grass shapes. The idea developed as I started to sketch a simple design and realized it looked like foliage, especially grasses. I liked the idea that quilting grasses would be something unexpected in a quilt of these colors. I pulled out a photo that I had taken of grasses and used it as my source of reference for the quilting. The quilting made for a unique fit with the colors and created a design on the quilt without distracting from the piecing; it became an integral part of the quilt.

See page 47 for tips on using tracing paper to find simple ideas that you can quilt.

Quilting: Use for inspiration or enlarge as desired.

See page 47 for tips on using tracing paper to find simple ideas that you can quilt.

tips & techniques

Using Value When Working With Solids

When you are working with solids, it is especially important to consider the values (lightness or darkness) of your fabrics. Using different colors provides some contrast, but those contrasts will really be apparent only when the values are different. Look at *Painted Grass* and see how the different values add movement to the quilt.

Using a value finder is one of the best ways to see values when selecting fabrics. For most fabrics use the red one, but for red fabrics use the green one. Be sure to have this valuable tool in your sewing room.

Use a value tool to make sure you have a range of values.

YARD SALE

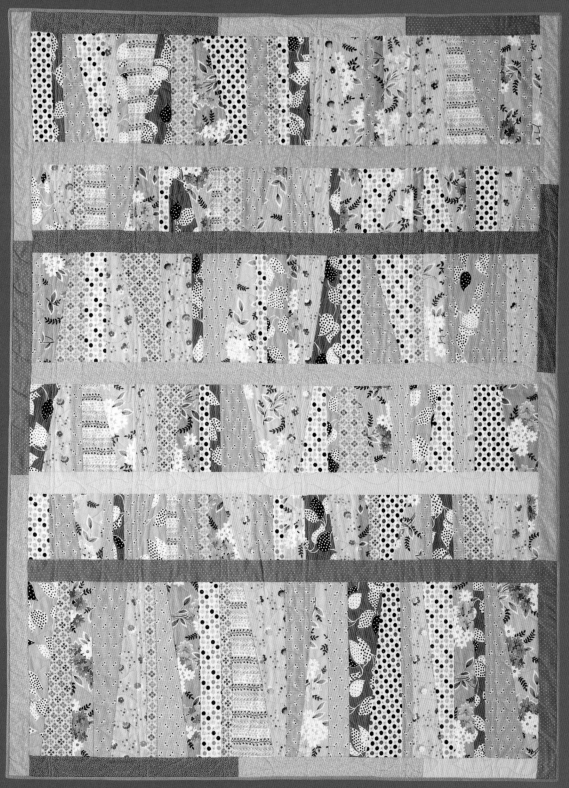

Finished size: 52″ × 70″

① **FABRIC:** Prints

② **PIECING:** Straight (creating wedges out of rectangles)

③ **QUILTING:** Fluid

The fabrics used in *Yard Sale* might have come from flea markets and yard sales, but they didn't. They are examples of a new '50s retro style of fabric that has become popular. My mother says they remind her of the style of fabric she learned to sew with.

Notice how the scale of the prints varies, making the design more interesting and moving the eye around the quilt. In particular, notice how the smaller scale of the border and sashing prints provides a quiet place for the eye to rest. Read more about creating a scrap-bag palette on page 42. Even though the prints are not really large scale, they are very interesting to work with—a nice change from the solids of *Painted Grass* (page 27).

This fabric collection caught my eye when it came into the shop. It made me think of summer—hanging out on the lawn with a good book, enjoying the day. Don't you love how fabric can evoke emotions and memories? Isn't it satisfying to weave those emotions into your quilts? What fabric will you use for your *Yard Sale*?

MATERIALS

Seventeen different fabrics are used for the rows of piecing and 5 different fabrics for the sashing. You may not find 17 fabrics that you like, so the total yardage amounts are included. Feel free to create your own Yard Sale. *Some of the rectangles will be cut on the crosswise grain rather than the lengthwise grain.*

- 4¼ yards total or ¼ yard each of 17 different prints for blocks

- 1¼ yards or ¼ yard each of 5 solid-like fabrics for sashing and borders

- 3⅛ yards for backing

- ⅝ yard for binding

- 56″ × 74″ batting

CUTTING AND SEWING

This quilt is made of angled wedges and rectangles. The illustrations show how to cut the wedges. I recommend cutting out the entire row of wedges and strips and then arranging them on a design wall before sewing them together. Refer to the Quilt Assembly Diagram on page 41.

SPECIAL CUTTING AND LABELING NOTE: Always place fabrics right side up when layering and cutting. Part of each rectangle will be discarded or can be used for another project. Follow the schematic, and place the ruler on the line indicated as the cutting line. Then pull apart the wedges, and place the "keeper" wedges together as shown. Label the pieces in each step.

ROW F CUTTING AND CONSTRUCTION

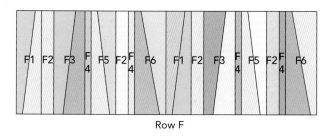

Row F

Begin with Row F because these large rectangles need to be cut on the crosswise grain using the ¼-yard cuts of fabric.

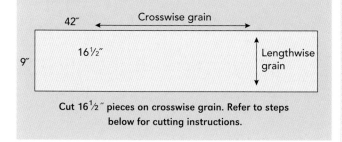

Cut 16½˝ pieces on crosswise grain. Refer to steps below for cutting instructions.

1. F1: Layer 4 fabrics right sides up, and cut a rectangle 3½˝ × 16½˝. Line up the ruler 1½˝ from the top right edge, angling to the bottom left corner. Cut as shown. Discard the A wedges. Combine the B wedges to make 2 rectangles.

Cut wedges for F1. Sew B wedges together.

2. F2: Layer 4 fabrics right sides up, and cut a rectangle 2½˝ × 16½˝.

3. F3: Layer 4 fabrics right sides up, and cut a rectangle 4˝ × 16½˝. Cut as shown. Discard the A wedges. Combine the B wedges to make 2 rectangles.

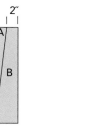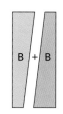

Cut wedges for F3. Sew B wedges together.

4. F4: Layer 4 fabrics right sides up, and cut a rectangle 1½˝ × 16½˝.

5. F5: Layer 4 fabrics right sides up, and cut a rectangle 3½˝ × 16½˝. Cut as shown. Discard the B wedges. Combine the A wedges to make 2 rectangles.

Cut wedges for F5. Sew A wedges together.

6. F6: Layer 4 fabrics right sides up, and cut a rectangle 4½˝ × 16½˝. Cut as shown. Discard the B wedges. Combine the A wedges to make 2 rectangles.

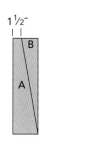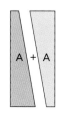

Cut wedges for F6. Sew A wedges together.

7. Refer to the Quilt Assembly Diagram, and arrange the pieces as indicated for Row F. Stitch the wedges and rectangles together. Press each seam. Set aside.

ROW E CUTTING AND CONSTRUCTION

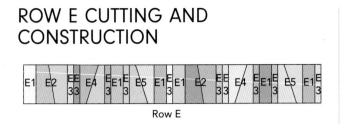

Row E

1. E1: Layer 6 fabrics right sides up, and cut a rectangle 2½" × 6½".

2. E2: Layer 4 fabrics right sides up, and cut a rectangle 3½" × 6½". Cut as shown. Discard the B wedges. Combine the A wedges to make 2 rectangles.

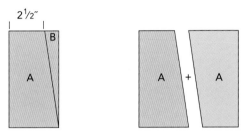

Cut wedges for E2. Sew A wedges together.

3. E3: Layer 10 fabrics right sides up, and cut a rectangle 1½" × 6½". If you don't have a fresh blade in your rotary cutter, make 2 stacks of 5.

4. E4: Layer 4 fabrics right sides up, and cut a rectangle 3½" × 6½". Cut as shown. Discard the A wedges. Combine the B wedges to make 2 rectangles.

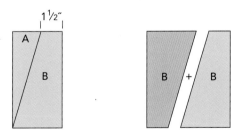

Cut wedges for E4. Sew B wedges together.

5. E5: Layer 4 fabrics right sides up, and cut a rectangle 3½" × 6½". Cut as shown. Discard the B wedges. Combine the A wedges to make 2 rectangles.

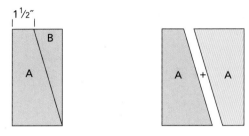

Cut wedges for E5. Sew A wedges together.

6. Refer to the Quilt Assembly Diagram, and arrange the pieces as indicated for Row E. Stitch the wedges and rectangles together. Press each seam. Set aside.

ROW D CUTTING AND CONSTRUCTION

Row D

1. D1: Layer 8 fabrics right sides up, and cut a rectangle 3½" × 8½". If you don't have a fresh blade in your rotary cutter, make 2 stacks of 4. Cut as shown. Discard the A wedges. Combine the B wedges to make 4 rectangles.

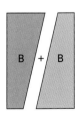

Cut wedges for D1. Sew B wedges together.

2. D2: Layer 6 fabrics right sides up, and cut a rectangle 1½" × 8½".

3. D3: Layer 4 fabrics right sides up, and cut a rectangle 4″ × 8½″. Cut as shown. Discard the B wedges. Combine the A wedges to make 2 rectangles.

Cut wedges for D3. Sew A wedges together.

4. D4: Layer 2 fabrics right sides up, and cut a rectangle 2½″ × 8½″.

5. D5: Layer 4 fabrics right sides up, and cut a rectangle 4½″ × 8½″. Cut as shown. Discard the B wedges. Combine the A wedges to make 2 rectangles.

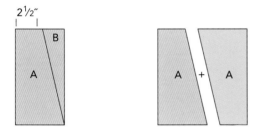

Cut wedges for D5. Sew A wedges together.

6. Refer to the Quilt Assembly Diagram, and arrange the pieces as indicated for Row D. Stitch the wedges and rectangles together. Press each seam. Set aside.

ROW C CUTTING AND CONSTRUCTION

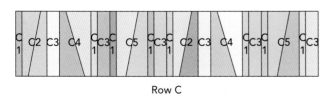

Row C

1. C1: Layer 8 fabrics right sides up, and cut a rectangle 1½″ × 10½″. If you don't have a fresh blade in your rotary cutter, make 2 stacks of 4.

2. C2: Layer 4 fabrics right sides up, and cut a rectangle 3½″ × 10½″. Cut as shown. Discard the A wedges. Combine the B wedges to make 2 rectangles.

Cut wedges for C2. Sew B wedges together.

3. C3: Layer 6 fabrics right sides up, and cut a rectangle 2½″ × 10½″.

4. C4: Layer 4 fabrics right sides up, and cut a rectangle 4½″ × 10½″. Cut as shown. Discard the B wedges. Combine the A wedges to make 2 rectangles.

Cut wedges for C4. Sew A wedges together.

5. C5: Layer 4 fabrics right sides up, and cut a rectangle 4″ × 10½″. Cut as shown. Discard the A wedges. Combine the B wedges to make 2 rectangles.

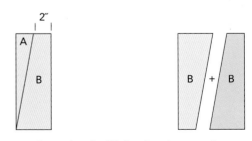

Cut wedges for C5. Sew B wedges together.

6. Refer to the Quilt Assembly Diagram, and arrange the pieces as indicated for Row C. Stitch the wedges and rectangles together. Press each seam. Set aside.

ROW B CUTTING AND CONSTRUCTION

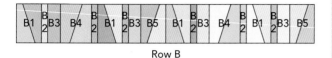

Row B

1. B1: Layer 8 fabrics right sides up, and cut a rectangle 3½˝ × 6½˝. If you don't have a fresh blade in your rotary cutter, make 2 stacks of 4. Cut as shown. Discard the B wedges. Combine the A wedges to make 4 rectangles.

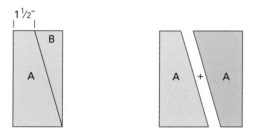

Cut wedges for B1. Sew A wedges together.

2. B2: Layer 6 fabrics right sides up, and cut a rectangle 1½˝ × 6½˝.

3. B3: Layer 4 fabrics right sides up, and cut a rectangle 2½˝ × 6½˝.

4. B4: Layer 4 fabrics right sides up, and cut a rectangle 4˝ × 6½˝. Cut as shown. Discard the A wedges. Combine the B wedges to make 2 rectangles.

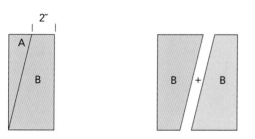

Cut wedges for B4. Sew B wedges together.

5. B5: Layer 4 fabrics right sides up, and cut a rectangle 3½˝ × 6½˝. Cut as shown. Discard the A wedges. Combine the B wedges to make 2 rectangles.

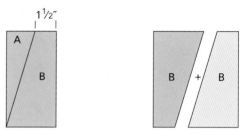

Cut wedges for B5. Sew B wedges together.

6. Refer to the Quilt Assembly Diagram, and arrange the pieces as indicated for Row B. Stitch the wedges and rectangles together. Press each seam. Set aside.

ROW A CUTTING AND CONSTRUCTION

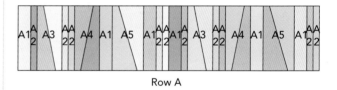

Row A

1. A1: Layer 6 fabrics right sides up, and cut a rectangle 2½˝ × 10½˝.

2. A2: Layer 10 fabrics right sides up, and cut a rectangle 1½˝ × 10½˝. If you don't have a fresh blade in your rotary cutter, make 2 stacks of 5.

3. A3: Layer 4 fabrics right sides up, and cut a rectangle 3½˝ × 10½˝. Cut as shown. Discard the B wedges. Combine the A wedges to make 2 rectangles.

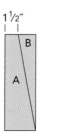
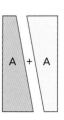

Cut wedges for A3. Sew A wedges together.

4. A4: Layer 4 fabrics right sides up, and cut a rectangle 3½" × 10½". Cut as shown. Discard the A wedges. Combine the B wedges to make 2 rectangles.

Cut wedges for A4. Sew B wedges together.

5. A5: Layer 4 fabrics right sides up, and cut a rectangle 4½" × 10½". Cut as shown. Discard the B wedges. Combine the A wedges to make 2 rectangles.

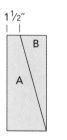

Cut wedges for A5. Sew A wedges together.

6. Refer to the Quilt Assembly Diagram, and arrange the pieces as indicated for Row A. Stitch the wedges and rectangles together. Press each seam. Set aside.

ASSEMBLY

SASHING AND BORDERS

1. Cut 3 strips 2½" × 42" from each of the 5 sashing and border fabrics. For each fabric, stitch 2 strips together, and cut to 48½" long for the sashing.

2. Arrange Rows A–F on a design wall with the sashing strips between the rows. Stitch the rows and sashing strips together. Press all the seams toward the sashing strips.

3. For the borders, cut the remaining 2½"-wide strips in half or as desired. A random look will work on this quilt. Sew the pieces together end-to-end as needed and cut the top and bottom borders 48½" long. Cut the side borders 70½" long.

4. Stitch the top and bottom borders to the quilt top, and press.

5. Stitch the side borders to the quilt top, and press.

FINISHING

1. Layer the backing, batting, and quilt top. Baste, and quilt as desired or use the quilting suggestion below.

2. Bind using your preferred method.

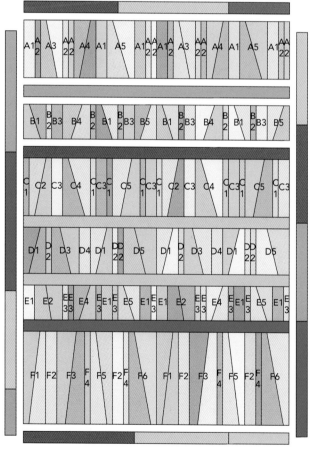

Quilt Assembly Diagram

FLUID QUILTING

Look to your prints for quilting inspiration. *Yard Sale* uses lots of them, and the challenge is to quilt in a way that adds to the overall design without competing with the prints or distracting from them. I found my quilting design in the leaf stripe in one of the prints. I chose this design because it would create long lines of simple shapes without taking away from the scrappy look of the quilt.

Quilting: Use for inspiration or enlarge as desired.

tips & techniques

Creating Scrap-Bag Palettes

When creating a scrap quilt, think about the size and scale of the prints.

1. Select a variety of prints that range from small to large designs and that range from compact and dense to loose and airy. Look at the swatches below and the *Yard Sale* quilt to see how the variety of scale in the prints adds interest to the quilt.

2. Be sure to use each print in several places—it keeps a scrap quilt from being too busy and helps move the eye around the quilt.

Look for a variety of prints when making scrap quilts.

BLOSSOM

Finished size: 42″ × 42″

1 **FABRIC:** Solid-like (hand dyes)

2 **PIECING:** Straight and blind-hem-stitch appliqué

3 **QUILTING:** Sketch

Blossom grew out of *The Red Tree* quilt design (page 49). After I had finished that quilt I thought about other ways of using the Nine-Patch design. A garden came to mind, with interpretations of flowers. I have been photographing flowers in gardens for years, so I started flipping through my pictures.

Have you ever noticed all the different shades of green in nature, and how well they always go with all the different colors of flowers? That's how the quilt began. As my mom says, "Green is nature's neutral." Once the greens were on the wall, the flower colors just seemed to come naturally.

I thought about the quilting as I was working on the piecing. *Blossom* had a specific direction from the beginning based on photographs of flowers. My first thought was that I could quilt realistic flowers in the circles, but as I stitched the quilt together I realized that something stylized would be more interesting.

I sketched and quilted the flowers and started to think about the foliage. The flowers were stylized, so why not stylize the foliage? In that way, I was able to add some straight lines that were organic, while the focus remained on the flowers.

See Tips and Techniques on page 47 for ideas on creating your own quilting designs. Even a simple quilt top with circles and squares can be stunning when you design your quilting to fit.

MATERIALS

Blossom is made from a variety of fabrics because I wanted each block to be different. To determine the yardage for your selection of fabrics, divide up the yardage based on the sizes of the squares and circles and the number of fabrics.

- 2⅜ yards total hand-dyed or other variegated fabrics for squares

- ⅞ yard total hand-dyed or other variegated fabrics for circles

- 1¼ yards for backing if the fabric is 45″ wide (otherwise, piece it horizontally; you will need 2½ yards)

- ⅜ yard for binding

- 46″ × 46″ batting

- Freezer paper

- Water-soluble gluestick

- Monofilament or invisible thread (smoke color for dark fabrics, clear for light fabrics)

CUTTING

Cut 9 squares 14½″ × 14½″.

PREPARING THE CIRCLES FOR APPLIQUÉ

1. Use a compass to draw 9 circles 9″ in diameter on freezer paper.

2. Refer to Preparing the Circles for Appliqué on page 51 to complete the appliqué preparation.

ASSEMBLY

1. Place the circles fabric side up in the centers of the squares. Pin in several places to secure while stitching.

2. Sew a blind-hem stitch around the edges of the circles with monofilament thread. Refer to Tips and Techniques on page 52 for instructions on blind-hem-stitch appliqué.

3. When you finish sewing each appliqué, trim away the background fabric from the backside, cutting ½″ inside the stitching line. Dampen the exposed freezer-paper pattern with water from a spray bottle to soften it, let it sit for 5 minutes, and then remove the paper. (See photo on page 51.) Press from both sides until the fabric is dry.

4. Arrange the squares and stitch them together in rows. Press the seam allowances in alternate directions for each row so the seams nest when you sew the rows together.

5. Stitch the rows together. Press.

FINISHING

1. Layer the backing, batting, and quilt top. Baste, and quilt as desired or use the quilting suggestion below.

2. Bind using your preferred method.

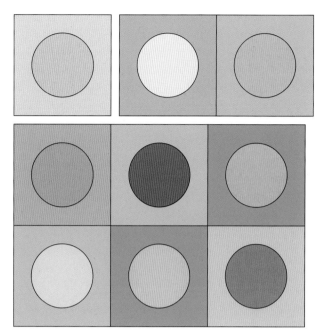

Quilt Assembly Diagram

SKETCH QUILTING

When you are quilting within a shape, you need to stylize your realistic design so it will fit the shape. If you are new to this type of quilting, practice on paper before sketching on your quilt. Try to design a different look for each flower, but make sure they all complement each other. See Tips and Techniques on page 47 for more ideas on creating your own quilting designs.

Keep your quilting loose and sketchy, and don't worry about stitching directly on the drawn lines. Add more lines of quilting with different colors of thread—one line of quilting can look tentative or sloppy, but when you add more, it develops an interesting character.

One of my favorite things about sketch quilting is what happens on the back when you use a solid fabric. When considering backing fabric, think about using a solid color so that your quilting design creates a wholecloth quilt. This makes a great two-sided quilt.

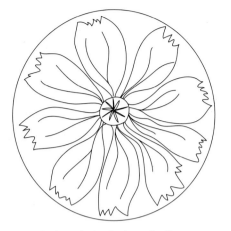

Quilting design for lavender flower

Quilting design for multicolored flower

Quilting design for yellow flower

Quilting design for pink flower

Quilting design for salmon red flower

Quilting design for red flower

Quilting design for turquoise flower

Quilting design for orange flower

Quilting design for purple flower

Back of *Blossom*

tips & techniques

Creating Quilting Designs

Here's a simple way to create your own quilting designs.

1. Look through books, magazines, or calendars to find a photo of a flower or design you like.

2. Simplify the image by placing tracing paper over the image and tracing the lines that you can see. Don't worry about the small details.

3. Use a photocopier to change the size to fit your quilt.

4. Cut out the copy, and use a gluestick to mount it on heavy paper. Then cut out the shape so you can use the heavy paper as a template.

5. Use a chalk pencil to trace around the design on the quilt top.

6. Quilt. Don't be afraid to go outside the lines—just use them as a guide.

THE RED TREE

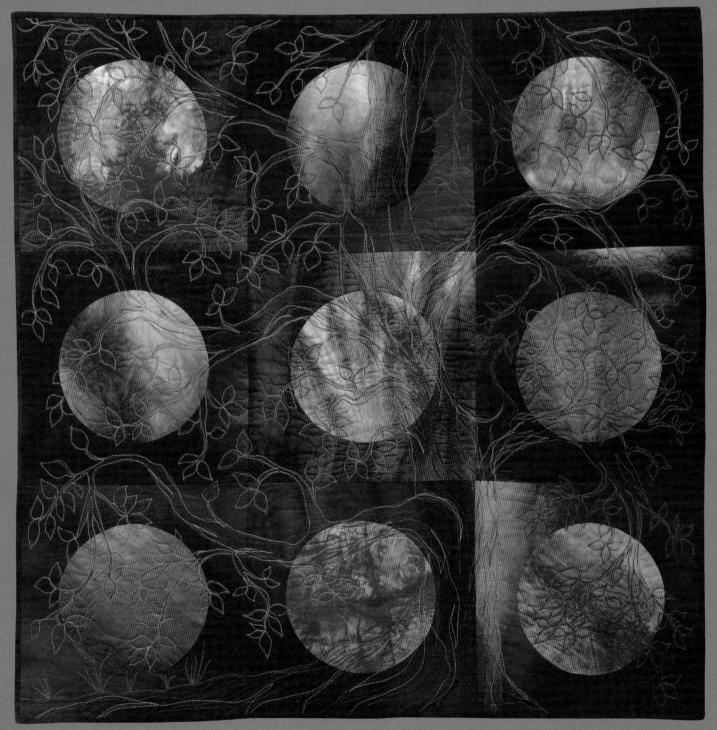

Finished size: 42″ × 42″

1 **FABRIC:** Solid-like (hand dyes)

2 **PIECING:** Straight and blind-hem-stitch appliqué

3 **QUILTING:** Sketch

The interesting aspect of this quilt is how it developed. Usually I am a planner, and when I create a top I have an idea for quilting in my mind as I piece. This time, I was searching for a creative spark. Reds seemed to keep coming up in my mind and in my photographs—all shades of red: cherry red, red-violet, fuchsia, pink, red-orange. As I looked through the images I had collected, I realized that a circular shape was repeated in all the photos. This was the start of the quilt.

I don't always have time to make an in-depth quilt with complicated piecing, and in this case I wanted some quick creative gratification. I pulled lots of red fabrics, searching for the right ones to express the feeling I had about red and the images. What stuck out the most were hand-dyed fabrics with rich variations in color. The darker areas of the fabric were used for the backgrounds, and the lighter sections for the circles. To attach the circles to the squares I used blind-hem-stitch machine appliqué. Voilà. I had a great top that fulfilled my red circle desire. Then it stayed on the design wall for months, waiting for quilting inspiration.

Quilting inspiration eluded me until I started looking at the trees around our house. They are juniper trees,

and some of them are so old that they are just trunks and branches with no foliage. As I looked through images of tree silhouettes, I started drawing on the quilt with a chalk pencil. After I had the basic structure, I realized that it needed leaves. Even though my inspiration was the silhouettes, I took artistic license and put leaves on the tree.

When I started quilting I was playing it really safe, using a color that matched the fabric. It felt blah, so I picked another color and started quilting over my first lines. This time I chose a brighter red; it started to make the quilting stand out. By the time I finished the quilting, I had used five different colors of thread. This quilting felt like sketching—the tree is not perfect but is sketched like a pencil drawing, only in thread.

Pick a color that inspires you. Gather fabric with different shades and values of that color, and make a quilt that speaks to you.

MATERIALS

The pictured quilt is made from a variety of fabrics because I wanted each block to be different. To determine the yardage for your selection of fabrics, divide up the yardage based on the size of the squares and circles and the number of fabrics.

- 2⅜ yards total hand-dyed or other variegated fabrics for squares

- ⅞ yard total hand-dyed or other variegated fabrics for circles

- 1¼ yards for backing if the fabric is 45″ wide (otherwise, piece it horizontally; you will need 2½ yards)

- ⅜ yard for binding

- 46″ × 46″ batting

- Freezer paper

- Water-soluble gluestick

- Monofilament or invisible thread (smoke color for dark fabrics, clear for light fabrics)

CUTTING

Cut 9 squares 14½″ × 14½″.

PREPARING THE CIRCLES FOR APPLIQUÉ

1. Use a compass to draw 9 circles 9″ in diameter on freezer paper.

2. Cut out the freezer-paper circles. Place the circles shiny side down on the wrong side of the fabric. Press with an iron until the freezer paper sticks to the fabric. Cut the fabric ¼″ beyond the edges of the freezer-paper templates. Do not remove the freezer paper.

3. Place the circles paper side up. It might be necessary to clip the edges of the circles to make folding the edges easier. Run a gluestick around the edges, catching both the edges of the freezer-paper templates and the fabric seam allowances. Use your fingertips to fold and finger-press the seam allowances onto the paper templates.

Fold seam allowance onto template.

ASSEMBLY

1. Place the circles fabric side up in the centers of the squares. Pin in several places to secure while stitching.

2. Sew a blind-hem stitch around the edges of the circles with monofilament thread. Refer to Tips and Techniques on page 52 for instructions on blind-hem-stitch appliqué.

3. When you finish sewing each appliqué, trim away the background fabric from the backside, cutting ½″ inside the stitching line. Dampen the exposed freezer-paper pattern with water from a spray bottle to soften it, let it sit for 5 minutes, and then remove the paper. Press from both sides until the fabric is dry.

Remove freezer-paper template, and press.

4. Arrange the squares, and stitch them together in rows. Press the seam allowances in alternate directions for each row so the seams nest when you sew the rows together.

5. Stitch the rows together. Press.

FINISHING

1. Layer the backing, batting, and quilt top. Baste, and quilt as desired or use the quilting suggestion below.

2. Bind using your preferred method.

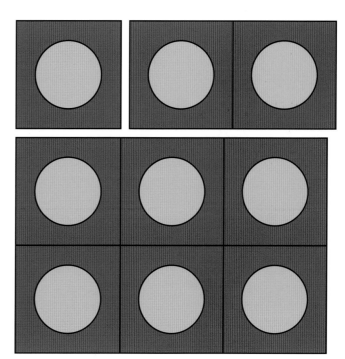

Quilt Assembly Diagram

SKETCH QUILTING

I have included a sketch that is similar to the tree on the quilt. I drew directly on the quilt, and as I quilted some of the lines changed.

Start with an outline in a thread color that is close to the color of the fabric. Then enhance those lines and work off them, increasing the intensity of the colors until you are satisfied.

Quilting: Use for inspiration or enlarge as desired.

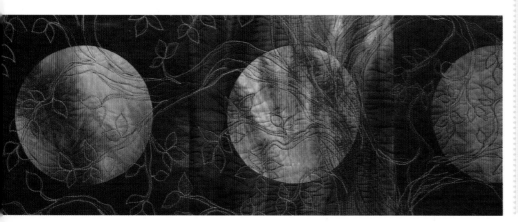

Using Blind-Hem-Stitch Appliqué

1. Select the blind-hem stitch on your sewing machine. Set the stitch width and length to 1mm or as short and narrow as possible on your machine.

2. Use a 60/8 embroidery needle.

3. Thread the machine with monofilament or invisible thread on top. Use clear monofilament or invisible thread on light fabric, and smoke on darker fabric.

4. Use 60-weight embroidery or bobbin thread in the bobbin.

5. Position the appliqué, and pin in place.

6. Practice stitching on scrap fabric to make sure the tension is correct and the stitch size is appropriate. Begin stitching with the needle close to the edge of the appliqué. If the gap between the needle and the appliqué is too wide, the zigzag won't be able to catch the edge of the appliqué when it hops over. Stitch carefully to make sure the stitch is catching the edge of the appliqué.

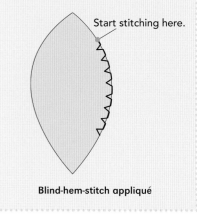

Start stitching here.

Blind-hem-stitch appliqué

ZINNIAS

Finished size: 60″ × 75″

1 **FABRIC:** Large-scale prints and solids

2 **PIECING:** Straight and blind-hem-stitch appliqué

3 **QUILTING:** Sketch

This colorful quilt illustrates how simple and wonderful large-scale prints can be. The colors in the zinnia fabrics (I used two different fabrics) provide all the cues you need to select the companion solids (see page 21 for tips on fabric selection). I selected eight different solid colors, but I could have used fewer if I had wanted one color to be more dominant.

This design grew out of the Nine-Patch design of *The Red Tree* (page 49). As the quilt got bigger, it became a better place to showcase large-scale prints. I alternated the solid fabrics with the large zinnia prints. Imagine the quilt with just the large circles. Now look at the photo and see how much more interesting it is with the addition of the small circles. Placing them in an irregular manner adds movement and interest.

Zinnias is a crossover in terms of quilting techniques. As with echo quilting, the design comes from the fabric, but the scale and style of quilting are more like the sketch technique. Be willing to experiment and try combining techniques. That will ensure that the quilt reaches its highest potential, and that you'll love it.

MATERIALS

- 3 yards total of large-scale theme prints for blocks
- 4 yards total or ½ yard each of 8 different solids for blocks
- 3¾ yards for backing
- ⅔ yard for binding
- 64″ × 79″ batting
- Freezer paper
- Washable gluestick
- Monofilament or invisible thread (smoke color for dark fabrics, clear for light fabrics)

CUTTING

Large-scale prints:

Cut 10 squares 15½″ × 15½″ for the blocks.

Solids:

Cut 10 squares 15½″ × 15½″ for the blocks.

PREPARING THE CIRCLES FOR APPLIQUÉ

1. Use a compass to draw 20 circles 10″ in diameter and 15 circles 4″ in diameter on freezer paper.

2. Refer to Preparing the Circles for Appliqué on page 51 to complete the appliqué preparation. Follow the instructions to prepare ten 10″ circles and five 5″ circles from the large-scale prints. Then prepare ten 10″ circles and ten 5″ circles from the solid colors.

ASSEMBLY

1. Place the 10″ print circles fabric side up in the centers of the solid squares. Pin in several places to secure while stitching. Place the 10″ solid circles in the centers of the print squares, and pin to secure while stitching.

2. Sew a blind-hem stitch around the edge of each circle with monofilament thread. Refer to Tips and Techniques on page 52 for instructions on blind-hem-stitch appliqué.

3. When you finish sewing each appliqué, trim away the background fabric, cutting ½″ inside the stitching line. Dampen the exposed freezer-paper pattern with water from a spray bottle to soften it, let it sit for 5 minutes, and then remove the paper. (See photo on page 51.) Press from both sides until the fabric is dry.

4. Repeat Steps 1–3 for the small circles, referring to the photograph for placement.

5. Refer to the Quilt Assembly Diagram to arrange the squares, and stitch them together in rows. Press the seam allowances in alternate directions for each row so the seams nest when you sew the rows together.

6. Stitch the rows together. Press.

FINISHING

1. Layer the backing, batting, and quilt top. Baste, and quilt as desired.

2. Bind using your preferred method.

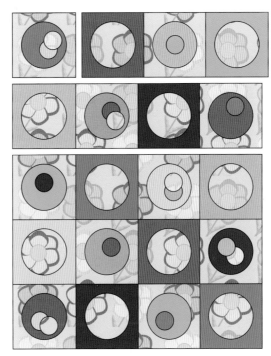

Quilt Assembly Diagram

SKETCH QUILTING

Although I would consider this sketch quilting, *Zinnias* was not as heavily quilted as *The Red Tree* or *Blossom*. The quilt didn't need the multiple threads to create an interesting design; the flower, being larger than life, created the interest. The print was mixed with solids, so it was important to make the quilting complement the floral design. I used a chalk pencil to sketch the flower on the quilt and then chose a thread color that was visible, but coordinated with the fabrics.

CIRCLE AROUND

Quilted by Lori Gailey. Finished size: 80″ × 92″

Photo by Sharon Risedorph

SIMPLE START—STUNNING FINISH

 FABRIC: Solids

2 PIECING: Straight and blind-hem-stitch appliqué

3 QUILTING: Echo

I like to set design challenges for myself, and using all solids was my mission for this quilt. As I sketched out different quilt ideas I realized that incorporating various sizes of squares and rectangles would create an interesting sense of movement within the quilt. Because all the fabrics are solids, this quilt became a color and value study.

Take a look at the quilt photo. Notice how the lighter-colored pieces look larger than the darker-colored pieces. Look at how the circles interact with the background and add another dimension. When you make a quilt like this, you need to audition the pieces, moving the colors around and playing with the placement of colors and shapes. If you don't have a design wall, use a bed or the floor. You can also work on this quilt in sections.

When it came time to quilt *Circle Around*, I knew it needed perfect circles. It would have been difficult for me to do that on my Bernina, so I asked my friend Lori Gailey, who is a professional longarm quilter, to work her magic on the quilt. She used my idea of repeating the circles to create movement.

Challenge yourself. Start with something simple like circles and squares, and see where it leads you.

MATERIALS

- ⅜ yard dark green for blocks
- ⅞ yard yellow-green for blocks and circles
- ¾ yard pink for blocks and circles
- ¾ yard light yellow for blocks and circles
- ½ yard dark yellow for blocks
- ⅜ yard royal blue for blocks and circles
- 1¾ yards red for blocks, circles, and binding
- 1 yard light blue for blocks and circles
- 1 yard lavender for blocks and circles
- ½ yard medium green for blocks and circles
- ⅞ yard orange for blocks and circle
- 1 yard light pink for blocks and circles
- ¾ yard purple for blocks and circles
- ½ yard yellow-orange for blocks and circle
- ⅝ yard dark blue for blocks and circle
- 7⅛ yards for backing
- 86″ × 98″ batting
- Freezer paper
- Water-soluble gluestick
- Monofilament or invisible thread (smoke color for dark fabrics, clear for light fabrics)

CUTTING

Refer to the Quilt Assembly Diagram on page 60.

Dark green:

Cut 1 rectangle 12½″ × 16½″ for A.

Cut 1 rectangle 9½″ × 20½″ for X.

Yellow-green:

Cut 1 square 16½″ × 16½″ for B.

Cut 1 rectangle 10½″ × 18½″ for R.

Cut 1 rectangle 12½″ × 18½″ for AA.

Pink:

Cut 1 rectangle 8½″ × 20½″ for D.

Cut 1 rectangle 14½″ × 18½″ for U.

Light yellow:

Cut 1 rectangle 16½″ × 20½″ for C.

Cut 1 square 12½″ × 12½″ for O.

Dark yellow:

Cut 1 rectangle 18½″ × 12½″ for W.

Cut 1 rectangle 11½″ × 16½″ for EE.

Royal blue:

Cut 1 rectangle 8½″ × 24½″ for E.

Red:

Cut 1 rectangle 8½″ × 16½″ for F.

Cut 1 square 20½″ × 20½″ for P.

Cut 1 rectangle 10½″ × 24½″ for HH.

Use the remaining piece for the binding.

Light blue:

Cut 1 rectangle 8½″ × 20½″ for G.

Cut 1 square 20½″ × 20½″ for Q.

Cut 1 rectangle 10½″ × 14½″ for GG.

Lavender:

Cut 1 rectangle 8½″ × 20½″ for H.

Cut 1 rectangle 12½″ × 24½″ for L.

Cut 1 rectangle 9½″ × 20½″ for Y.

Cut 1 rectangle 8½″ × 22½″ for CC.

Medium green:

Cut 1 square 14½″ × 14½″ for I.

Cut 1 rectangle 12½″ × 16½″ for N.

Orange:

Cut 1 square 14½″ × 14½″ for J.

Cut 1 rectangle 12½″ × 28½″ for M.

Light pink:

Cut 1 rectangle 10½″ × 28½″ for K.

Cut 1 rectangle 12½″ × 18½″ for BB.

Purple:

Cut 1 rectangle 9½″ × 16½″ for S.

Cut 1 rectangle 16½″ × 24½″ for Z.

Yellow-orange:

Cut 1 rectangle 9½″ × 16½″ for T.

Cut 1 square 14½″ × 14½″ for FF.

Dark blue:

Cut 1 rectangle 8½″ × 18½″ for V.

Cut 1 rectangle 11½″ × 16½″ for DD.

CIRCLE APPLIQUÉS

1. For the circle appliqués, use a compass to draw circles with the following diameters on the dull side of the freezer paper, and use a permanent marker to label each template. Draw:

- one 12″ circle (label as #11 lavender)

- one 11½″ circle (#17 royal blue)

- one 11″ circle (#2 yellow-orange)

- one 10½″ circle (#19 pink)

- two 10″ circles (#5 purple and #15 lavender)

- five 8″ circles (#3 red, #4 light pink, #8 dark blue, #12 light yellow, and #18 light yellow)

- three 7″ circles (#16 medium green, #21 light pink, and #22 red)

- eight 6″ circles (#1 purple, #6 yellow-green, #7 light blue, #9 light blue, #10 pink, #13 royal blue, #14 orange, and #20 light blue)

2. Refer to Preparing the Circles for Appliqué on page 51, and follow the instructions to prepare the circles. Match the freezer-paper templates to the fabric colors. Keep the label numbers showing.

3. Set these aside to add after each section is assembled.

ASSEMBLY

Refer to the Quilt Assembly Diagram to lay out the quilt. You will assemble it section by section.

1. To assemble **Section 1**:

Sew A to the top of B; press.

Stitch C to the left side of D; press.

Stitch E to the bottom of C/D; press.

Stitch A/B to the left side of C/D/E; press.

2. Refer to the Quilt Assembly Diagram for placement of Circles #1 and #2. Follow the blind-hem-stitch appliqué instructions on page 52 to sew the circles to the quilt. Circle #3 will be added in Step 4.

3. When you finish sewing each appliqué, trim away the background fabric, cutting in ½˝ from the stitching line. Dampen the exposed freezer-paper pattern with water from a spray bottle to soften it, let it sit for 5 minutes, and then remove the paper. (See photo on page 51.) Press from both sides until the fabric is dry.

4. If you are layering 2 circles, add the larger one to the quilt first, and then add the smaller circle. Repeat Steps 2 and 3 to add Circle #3 to Section 1. Trim away the background fabric of the second circle as you did before.

5. Continue assembling the sections as follows, repeating Steps 2 and 3 to add the circles to each section.

Section 2:

Stitch G to the left side of H; press.

Stitch F to the top of G/H; press.

Stitch I to the top of J; press.

Stitch K to the left side of I/J; press.

Stitch F/G/H to the left side of I/J/K; press.

Section 3:

Stitch O to the bottom of N; press.

Stitch M to the left side of O/N; press.

Stitch L to the top of M/N/O; press.

Stitch P to the top of Q; press.

Stitch L/M/N/O to the left side of P/Q; press.

Section 4:

Stitch S to the left side of T; press.

Stitch U to the bottom of S/T; press.

Stitch R to the top of S/T/U; press.

Stitch X to the left side of Y; press.

Stitch W to the bottom of V; press.

Stitch X/Y to the bottom of V/W; press.

Section 5:

Stitch AA to the top of BB; press.

Stitch Z to the left side of AA/BB; press.

Section 6:

Stitch DD to the left side of EE; press.

Stitch CC to the top of DD/EE; press.

Stitch FF to the top of GG; press.

Stitch HH to the right side of FF/GG; press.

Stitch CC/DD/EE to the left side of FF/GG/HH.

6. Join the sections into rows. Then join the rows.

7. Look at the photograph to position the last circle. Add Circle #22 on the seam between the middle and bottom rows.

FINISHING

1. Layer the backing, batting, and quilt top. Baste, and quilt as desired.

2. Bind using your preferred method.

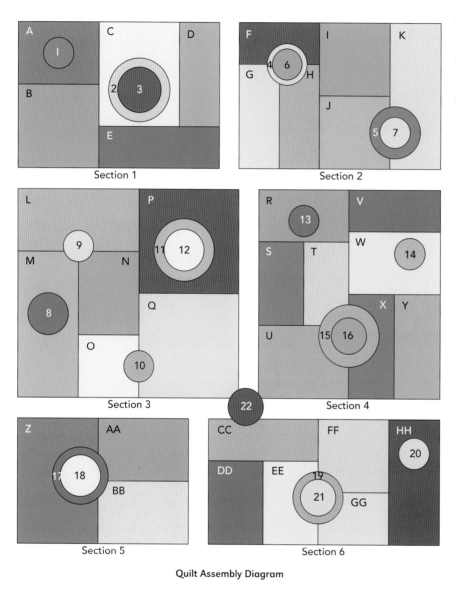

Section 1

Section 2

Section 3

Section 4

Section 5

Section 6

Quilt Assembly Diagram

ECHO QUILTING

Quilt circles to echo the appliquéd circles. Let them overlap and intersect to add even more depth. It is a playful way to create movement and dimension on the quilt without adding more fabric circles.

tips & techniques

Adding Interest by Varying the Design Elements

Quilts that have too much going on are hard to look at. Quilts that don't have enough going on aren't very interesting. An easy way to add complexity to a quilt without making it overwhelming is to use simple design elements (such as shape and color) and vary some aspect of the elements.

1. Use simple shapes such as squares, rectangles, or circles, and vary the size and/or placement.

2. Use a variety of colors while maintaining some element of consistency, such as using all solid colors.

3. Use a variety of values so the design elements contrast with the surrounding fabrics.

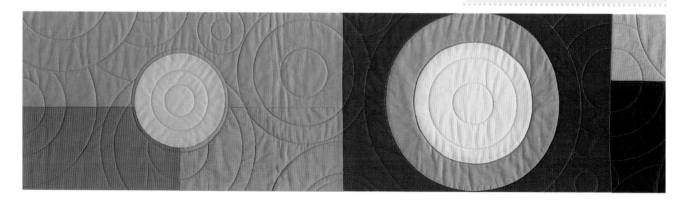

EFFERVESCENCE

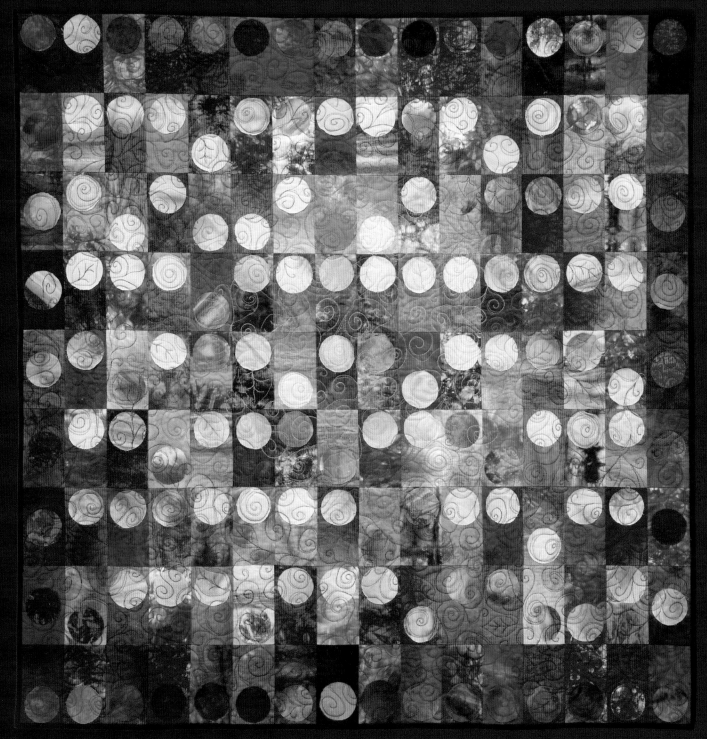

Finished size: 48″ × 49½″

① **FABRIC:** Solid-like (hand dyes)

② **PIECING:** Straight and raw-edge appliqué

③ **QUILTING:** Fluid

Inspiration comes from many sources, and it is always amazing to me where I can find simple design ideas and inspiration for quilts and fabric.

The idea for *Effervescence* came from a TV commercial. The commercial showed litmus papers with thumbprints on them lined up in a grid. They were rectangles with oblong circles. For some reason this graphic stuck with me, and a few months later when I wanted to make something—something beautiful that could just be for me—that graphic image came to mind. I pulled out some hand-dyed fabrics that were in my stash just waiting to be used, and started cutting rectangles.

It was spring in Sisters where I live, and the grasses and bushes were in bloom, enhancing the color of the high desert. The colors I found myself using for *Effervescence* were similar to those of the landscape that surrounded my house, but just a bit more intense. I didn't have a

plan for the quilt until I had quite a few of the rectangles up on the wall. I realized that I could use lighter values of the rectangle colors for the circles, and darker values for the border, which I wanted to be subtle.

After all the circles were cut out and placed, I had to decide how to attach them. Fusing them to the rectangles was an easy solution—I planned the quilt to be a wall-hanging that I wouldn't wash, so I decided to leave the circles raw edged.

Effervescence shows that you don't always have to have a plan when you begin a quilt. See page 64 for more ideas on following your inspiration.

MATERIALS

Use a variety of fabrics, watching the values.

- 1⅝ yards total medium-value fabrics for center rectangles

- 1 yard total dark-value fabrics for outside rectangles (These fabrics are a little darker than the center rectangle fabrics.)

- ⅝ yard total light-value fabrics for center circles (These fabrics are lighter than the center rectangle fabrics.)

- ⅓ yard total darker-value fabrics for outside circles (These fabrics are darker than the outside rectangle fabrics.)

- ½ yard for binding

- 3 yards for backing

- 52″ × 54″ batting

- 1 yard fusible web

CUTTING

Medium values:

Cut 98 rectangles 3½" × 6" for the center rectangles.

Dark values:

Cut 46 rectangles 3½" × 6" for the outside rectangles.

Light values:

Cut 98 circles 2½" in diameter for the center circles.

Darker values:

Cut 46 circles 2½" in diameter for the outside circles.

Fusible web: Cut 144 squares 2" × 2".

ASSEMBLY

1. On a design wall or a flat surface, arrange 16 of the outside darker rectangles to create the first row. In the next row, place 1 dark rectangle, then 14 center rectangles, and end with 1 dark rectangle. Repeat this row until there are 8 rows, including the first dark row. The last row will be all dark. Refer to the Quilt Assembly Diagram and the quilt photo as needed.

2. Iron the fusible-web squares to the circles of fabric. Peel off the paper. Because the sizes of the fabric circles and the fusible web are different, the loose raw fabric wedges will add dimension and interest to the finished quilt.

3. Place 1 circle on each rectangle. Notice the placement of the circles on the rectangles. On the outside edges, the circles are placed at the tops of the rectangles at the top of the quilt, in the middle of the rectangles on the sides of the quilt, and at the bottoms of the rectangles at the bottom of the quilt. In the center, the circles are predominantly at the tops of the rectangles, but there are a few at the bottom to add interest. Play with the placement of the circles until you get the desired look. Now fuse the circles onto the rectangles.

4. Stitch the rectangles together in rows. Press the seam allowances in alternate directions for each row so the seams nest when you sew the rows together.

5. Stitch the rows together.

FINISHING

1. Layer the backing, batting, and quilt top. Baste, and quilt as desired or use the quilting suggestion below. When you are quilting over the raw edges, be sure to take your time so none of the circle edges get folded over. Some of the edges of the circle may fray a bit, but this will add another texture to the quilt.

2. Bind using your preferred method.

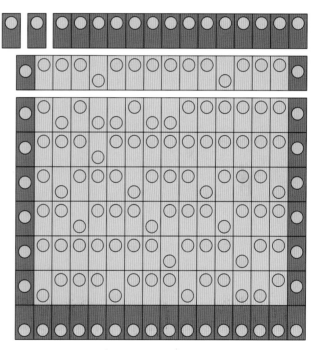

Quilt Assembly Diagram

FLUID QUILTING

Fluid quilting is subtle and becomes a part of the quilt without distracting from the movement of the colors. One of my favorite designs for this type of quilting is a swirl. Swirls are easy and are created in a continuous line so you don't have those pesky threads to cut.

Start with a light thread color, and work your way to the middle of the quilt creating swirls. Add a few leaves here and there. Work your way outward in a circular design. Change thread colors following the colors and values of the quilt, starting with a light color and moving to darker colors by the time you get to the outside of the quilt.

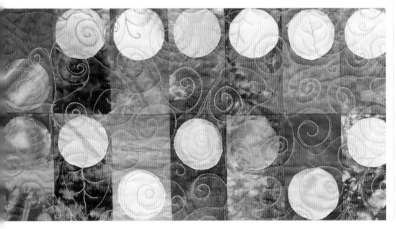

Quilting: Use for inspiration or enlarge as desired.

CERULEAN SANDS

Finished size: 48″ × 20″

1 **FABRIC:** Solid-like

2 **PIECING:** Straight, simple curves, and blind-hem-stitch appliqué

3 **QUILTING:** Fluid

Is there anything more inspiring than a trip to the beach? During my last trip to the beach I took time to think about what I was seeing, in addition to enjoying the experience of being there.

As in any other landscape, the colors on the beach shift during the day as the light changes and the clouds move in the sky. The blues of the ocean coupled with the colors of sand were the inspiration for this simple curve-pieced landscape study. Gentle curves emerge in the water and carry through the sand to the sand dunes. I started sketching and thinking about how I could design a quilt to reflect what I was seeing. My mother had taught me how to cut and sew simple curves, and I like the results of this kind of freestyle piecing.

Placing the landscape in a circle is a way to capture the feeling of the sun setting over the horizon. The subtle changes in light from morning to noon to night are reflected in the three circles.

This quilt was also a lesson in the power of repetition (page 55) and combining design elements (page 68).

MATERIALS

- 1¼ yards total of a variety of blues for landscapes (The border uses ½ yard; the rest of the blues can be scraps, or purchase ⅛-yard cuts.)

- 1 yard beige or 3 squares 14½″ × 14½″ of different fabrics for background

- ¼ yard beige for landscapes

- 1½ yards for backing

- ⅓ yard for binding

- 52″ × 24″ batting

- Freezer paper

- Water-soluble gluestick

- Monofilament or invisible thread (smoke color for dark fabrics, clear for light fabrics)

CUTTING

Beige:

Cut 3 squares 14½″ × 14½″ for the background blocks.

Cut the landscape pieces as you piece.

Blue:

Cut 4 strips 3½″ × 42″. Sew the strips together into 1 long strip. From this, cut 2 pieces 20½″ long for the side borders, and cut 2 pieces 42½″ long for the top and bottom borders.

Cut the landscape pieces as you piece.

ASSEMBLY

SIMPLE CURVE PIECING

If you have never done this style of piecing you might want to try out the technique on a small sample. You will love how this technique opens up new doors for you; think of it as another technique to put in your quilt design toolbox.

1. Use a compass to draw 3 circles 9″ in diameter on freezer paper. Cut out the circles.

2. Determine the finished size of the landscapes within the circles, which in this case is 9″. Add a 1″ working seam allowance to this while you are piecing; you will be working with strips that measure 10″ in length. Set a 9″-circle freezer-paper pattern beside you as you work so you can see how much space you are filling as you cut, and sew the pieces.

3. Lay out the fabrics in the order you think will look best for each circle, taking into consideration that you will see less of the pieces at the top and bottom because of the curve. It's a good idea to include some of the background fabric in each circle; this will help integrate the circles with the background.

4. Begin at the top of one circle, and cut a rectangle 10″ long and 1½″ wider than you think you want to use in the circle. Cut a second rectangle for the next piece. Layer the second rectangle on top of the first, overlapping them by 1½″, with the right sides of the fabrics up.

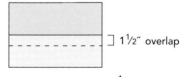

Overlap fabric 1½″.

5. Cut a gentle curve with the rotary cutter through the layered fabrics. Be sure to keep the cut within the 1½″ overlap. Remove the excess fabric and you have 2 pieces of fabric that fit together.

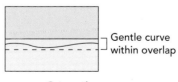

Cut gentle curve.

6. Place the 2 pieces right sides together, matching the raw edges at the left end. This may seem awkward, but don't worry; you'll trim the edges later. Do not try to pin all the edges together. They will ease in just fine. Use a scant ¼″ seam allowance, and stitch the 2 pieces together. Just work an inch at a time, matching the raw edges. You will find yourself easing the top fabric some of the time, and other times you'll need to ease the bottom fabric. If there is a deep curve it can be clipped, but clip in only ⅛″. This will open up the curve so the 2 raw edges match up more easily. Only clip the fabric on an inside curve as shown.

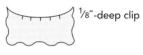

Make ⅛″ clips if needed.

7. Continue with this technique until you have made a square at least 10″ × 10″. Press the seams in one direction. I like to press them toward the bottom of the landscape.

8. Repeat Steps 4–7 for the other 2 circles.

APPLIQUÉD CIRCLES

1. Refer to Preparing the Circles for Appliqué on page 51, and follow the instructions to prepare the circles.

2. Center each circle fabric side up on a background block. Refer to Using Blind-Hem-Stitch Appliqué (page 52) for instructions to sew the circles to the blocks.

3. When you finish sewing each appliqué, trim away the background fabric, cutting in ½" from the stitching line. Dampen the exposed freezer-paper pattern with water from a spray bottle to soften it, let it sit for 5 minutes, and then remove the paper. (See photo on page 51.) Press from both sides until the fabric is dry.

FINAL ASSEMBLY

1. Stitch the 3 blocks together. Press.

2. Add the top and bottom borders, then the sides. Press.

FINISHING

1. Layer the backing, batting, and quilt top. Baste, and quilt as desired.

2. Bind using your preferred method.

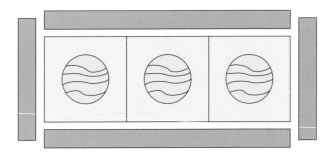

Quilt Assembly Diagram

FLUID QUILTING

For the quilting pattern for *Cerulean Sands* I used the landscape as inspiration. The gentle curves create a simple quilting line that is carried throughout the design. Taking your quilting cues from the piecing can enhance the quilt without taking away from the design.

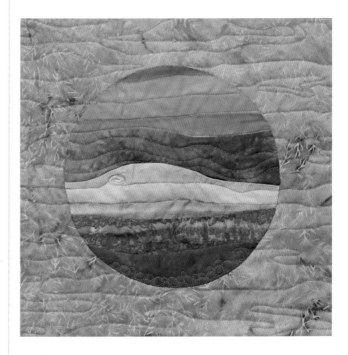

tips & techniques

Combining Design Elements

Combining two or more elements that have something in common can make for an interesting design. In *Cerulean Sands*, the gentle curve piecing complements the circular shapes and adds movement to an almost "too simple" design. The quilting then mimics the gentle curves in the background, repeating the design element. *Coming Home* (next page) uses the same shapes and techniques but creates a more complex quilt by using the squares as a foundation for the circles. This adds another design element, but because all the squares are in the same color family there is continuity. When combining design elements, make sure they support each other harmoniously and don't compete too much for attention.

COMING HOME

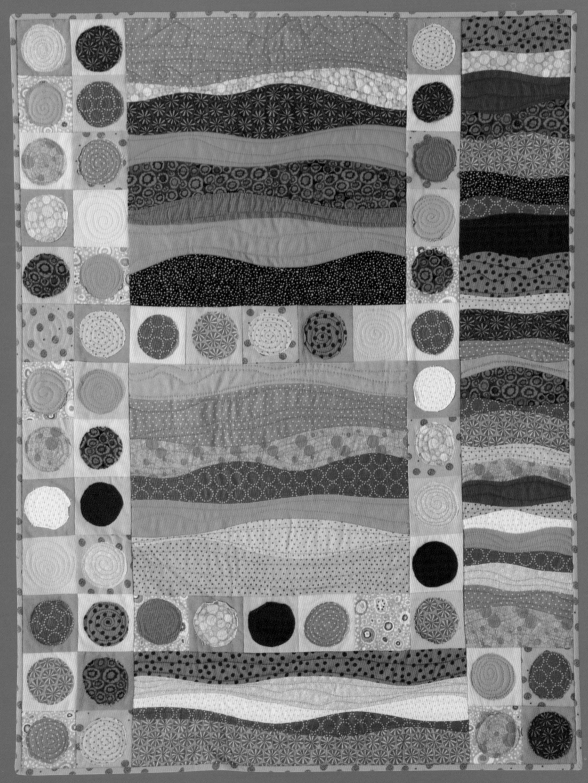

Finished size: 30″ × 39″

Colors change with the seasons, but the landscape lines are always the same. The simple curve piecing technique is the perfect piecing choice for this quilt. I love how the circles add texture and layers to a quilt. This design creates a combination of straight lines and curves with circles as accents, and the raw-edge appliqué adds a rustic touch to the quilt. Read more about using accents on page 73.

① **FABRIC:** Solid-like and prints

② **PIECING:** Straight, simple curves, and raw-edge appliqué

③ **QUILTING:** Fluid

I have a beautiful six-mile drive from my home to Sisters, Oregon. The landscape changes from juniper trees to ponderosa pines, with meadows and wild-flowers alongside the road. Then there are the majestic Three Sisters mountains, with the foothills below. I grew up in Sisters, and I think I could sketch this landscape in my head.

The colors of late summer inspired the palette for this quilt. The dots and dot-like fabrics reflect the bright colors of the meadows, along with the gold that is starting to appear in the landscape. Most of the snow has melted from the mountaintops.

MATERIALS

Notice the proportion of colors from each color family of purple, blue, green, red, and yellow. There are more golds, purples, and greens, so the reds and blues become accents. When selecting your fabrics, pick 3 color families as your main colors and 2 colors as accents. Select an assortment from each color family, but remember to use each fabric in several places.

- ⅓ yard total of purples for circles and curved strips
- ½ yard total of greens for circles and curved strips
- ⅓ yard total of blues for circles and curved strips
- ¼ yard total of reds for circles and curved strips
- ⅛ yard total of yellows for circles and curved strips
- ¼ yard gold for circles and curved strips
- ¼ yard each of 3 different golds for squares
- 1½ yards for backing and binding
- 34″ × 43″ batting
- ¼ yard paper-backed fusible web

CUTTING

Gold:

Cut a total of 5 strips 3½″ wide. From these cut 51 squares 3½″ × 3½″.

Cut the remainder of the pieces as you compose your project.

ASSEMBLY

1. On a design wall or a flat surface, arrange the gold squares as indicated on the Quilt Assembly Diagram and in the quilt photo.

2. Refer to the instructions on page 67 for simple curve piecing. Cut the rectangles 1″ longer than the finished blocks. Be sure to cut the rectangles wide enough so that you allow plenty of room for cutting the curves. Refer to the photograph to plan your blocks. I suggest that you cut all the rectangles for all the pieced sections and put them on the design wall before sewing anything. That way you can make sure the colors are balanced in the overall design. When you like the arrangement of colors, make the cuts, and sew the gentle curves. Continue piecing each block so it is 1″ wider than the finished block will be. You will trim the blocks later.

In this quilt I started with the blues and purples in the top block, then I worked down to the grassy meadow colors. Red pops in periodically, adding an accent to the quilt.

3. After the landscape blocks are complete, trim each block as follows:

Block 1: 15½″ × 15½″

Block 2: 15½″ × 12½″

Block 3: 18½″ × 6½″

Block 4: 6½″ × 33½″

4. Refer to the Quilt Assembly Diagram, stitch each section together, and press. Stitch the sections together as follows:

Stitch Section A to Section B; press.

Stitch C to A/B; press.

Stitch D to the left side of A/B/C; press.

Stitch E to the right side of A/B/C/D; press.

5. Cut 46 circles with a 2½″ diameter, or cut the circles freehand as I did. Place all the circles in position before fusing them to the gold squares. Make sure the colors are balanced. Cut a 1¼″ × 1¼″ square of fusible web for each circle, and fuse it to the back of the circle. Peel off the paper, and fuse the circles in the centers of the gold squares. The loose raw edges of the circles will give this quilt some dimension and add more interest.

FINISHING

1. Layer the backing, batting, and quilt top. Baste, and quilt as desired or use the quilting suggestion below.

2. Bind using your preferred method.

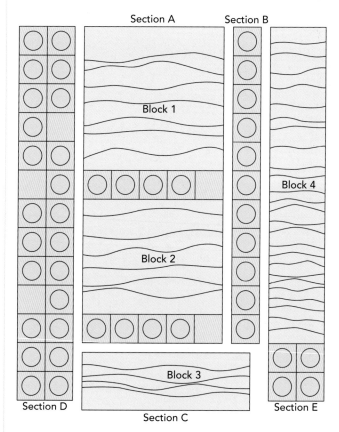

Quilt Assembly Diagram

FLUID QUILTING

Coming Home was simple to quilt. The lines and shapes in the piecing provide the quilting lines that enhance the design without distracting from the prints or the piecing. Follow the lines in the landscape areas, using the gentle curves as a guide. For the circles, start in the middle, and spiral out to the edge. There are times when you just don't need much quilting to make the quilt work.

Begin quilting design in center of circle.

Using Accents

One technique to make sure a quilt is interesting is to use some of the elements of the quilt in different proportions. Accents can achieve the desired effect in two ways.

1. Use color as an accent: Determine which colors or fabrics are the predominant colors, and use other colors sparingly.

2. Use shape as an accent: Add a shape that is different from the predominant shapes in a quilt, such as adding circles to straight and gently curved lines.

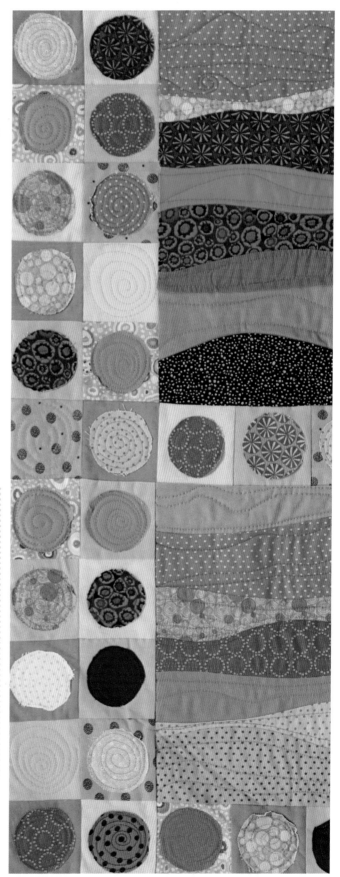

FIREFLY

Finished size: 47″ × 52″

1   **FABRIC:** Solid-like and large-scale theme print

2   **PIECING:** Straight and paper-foundation piecing

3   **QUILTING:** Echo

Classic New York Beauties inspire me. I love to make New York Beauty quilts, and designing the blocks is a fun way to push the limits of the traditional. The block in *Firefly* is designed with long shapes to really show off the pointed Beauty blocks that are paper-foundation pieced. (For tips and techniques on paper-foundation piecing, see page 82).

The large-scale dahlia fabric was the inspiration for the design. I tried to use it in the blocks, but the large-scale print just didn't work in the New York Beauty piecing. However, it does work beautifully in the sashing and filler areas. Any large-scale theme print will work for this design. The key is to pick a fabric that has lights and darks in it to coordinate with the New York Beauty blocks. Be sure to select a good range of light and dark solid-like fabrics to create contrast within the block. And notice how there is a mix of the theme print and solids in the filler areas to create unity between the blocks and the filler space.

Firefly grew out of a love of New York Beauties and large-scale prints, and emerged as an exploration of color and design. If you want another New York Beauty–style quilt, try *Lily Pond*, starting on page 89. You'll also find more New York Beauties in my book *Radiant New York Beauties* (see page 95).

MATERIALS

- 1⅛ yards large-scale theme print for rectangles and outer border

- ⅓ yard each of 2 different darks for filler blocks and inner border

- ⅜ yard each of 5 different darks for arc centers and points

- ⅜ yard each of 7 different medium brights for arc centers and points

- ½ yard for binding

- 2⅞ yards for backing

- 51″ × 56″ batting

- Foundation paper for arcs (see Resources on page 95)

- Tape for putting arc papers together

- 3″ × 15″ rectangle of template plastic

- Optional: Add-a-Quarter ruler

CUTTING

Large-scale theme print:

Cut 3 strips 5½″ × 42″ for the filler blocks. From
   these cut:

- 6 rectangles 2½″ × 5½″
- 4 rectangles 3½″ × 5½″
- 1 rectangle 4½″ × 5½″
- 5 squares 5½″ × 5½″
- 2 rectangles 5½″ × 7½″
- 1 rectangle 5½″ × 8½″
- 2 rectangles 5½″ × 9½″

Cut 5 strips 3″ × 42″. Stitch these together for the outside border, and cut 4 strips 3″ × 47½″ long.

Darks (⅓-yard cuts):

From 1 dark fabric, cut 3 strips 1½″ × 42″. Stitch these
   together, and cut 2 strips 42½″ long for the top and
   bottom inner borders.

From the other dark fabric, cut 3 strips 1½″ × 42″.
   Stitch these together, and cut 2 lengths 45½″ for
   the side inner borders.

Cut 1 strip 1½″ × 42″ from each of 2 darks. From
   these, cut 13 rectangles 1½″ × 5½″ for the
   filler blocks.

Darks (⅜-yard cuts):

*Use the template patterns on page 87. Make copies,
enlarging as indicated. This is easiest to do on
a copy machine.*

Template A: Cut 2 pieces. Use a different fabric for
   each piece. Mark your fabric where the black dot is.
   This is a matching point for joining the arc.

Template Ar: Cut 2 pieces. Use a different fabric for
   each piece. Mark your fabric where the black dot is.
   This is a matching point for joining the arc.

Cut the remaining dark fabrics into strips 4¼″ × 42″ for
   piecing the arcs.

Medium brights:

*Use the template patterns on page 87. Make copies,
enlarging as indicated. This is easiest to do on a copy
machine.*

Template A: Cut 2 pieces. Use a different fabric for
   each piece. Mark your fabric where the black dot is.
   This is a matching point for joining the arc.

Template Ar: Cut 2 pieces. Use a different fabric for
   each piece. Mark your fabric where the black dot is.
   This is a matching point for joining the arc.

After cutting the patterns from the templates, use the
   fabric scraps to cut 14 rectangles 1½″ × 5½″ for
   the filler blocks.

Cut the remaining medium-bright fabrics into strips
   4¼″ × 42″ for piecing the arcs.

ASSEMBLY

PREPARATION

1. Use the patterns on pages 83–86 to make 4 copies
of each set of arcs onto foundation paper, enlarging as
indicated. This is easiest to do using a copy machine.
There is 1 arc facing right and 1 facing left. Tape the 2
halves of each arc together, matching up the stitching
lines. The block will measure 10½″ × 15½″ with seam
allowances. Trim the excess paper ¼″ beyond the
block pattern. **Note: Make sure the tape is NOT on a
stitching line.**

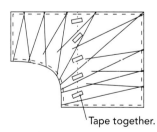

Tape together.

Block will measure 10½″ × 15½″.

2. Place the dark-colored 4¼″-wide strips in a pile and the medium-bright 4¼″ strips in another pile. You will make 4 blocks with dark backgrounds and bright points and 4 blocks with bright backgrounds and dark points. Two of each color will be facing left and 2 of each will be facing right. Decide which you will start with. The arc patterns have the point sections marked with a P.

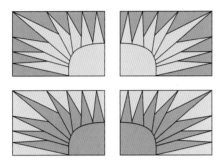

Make 2 of each arc.

3. Set the machine stitch length to 1.5, or 18 stitches to the inch, for paper-foundation piecing. (This will help prevent distortion when tearing off the paper.)

PIECING THE ARCS

1. Lay the edge of the template plastic on the line between the #1 and #2 sections of the arc pattern (the first line of stitching), and fold the pattern on the line to crease the pattern against the template plastic. This will make it easier to remove the paper later.

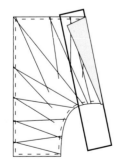

Fold paper against template plastic.

2. Place a dark strip and a bright strip right sides together, with the background fabric on top and the point fabric underneath. Place the folded-back pattern edge on the fabrics, leaving a ¼″ seam allowance to the left of the fold as shown.

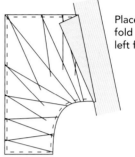

Place pattern fold ¼″ from left fabric edge.

Position fabric and paper for stitching.

3. Fold the paper back, and put 2 or 3 pins through the paper and fabric.

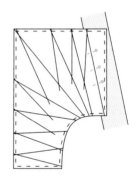

Pin first piece to hold fabric and paper together.

4. Stitch through the paper on the line, stitching past the seam allowances at each end. Open the 2 fabrics, and finger-press. If the fabrics are stubborn, use an iron. Trim just the background fabric to ¼″ beyond the edge of the paper.

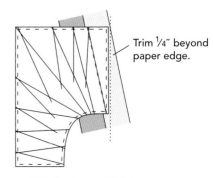

Trim ¼″ beyond paper edge.

Trim background fabric.

5. Place the template plastic on the second stitching line for section 2, and fold back the paper. Now you can trim the point fabric to ¼″ beyond the folded edge of the paper.

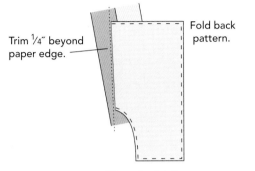

Trim ¼″ beyond paper edge.

Fold back pattern.

Trim point fabric.

6. With the pattern still folded back, choose a second background fabric, and place it right sides together with the arc fabric, lining up the raw edges as shown. Fold the paper back over, and pin as you did above. Stitch to the bottom of the printed line. **DO NOT** stitch to the bottom of the block, or you will get too much excess fabric.

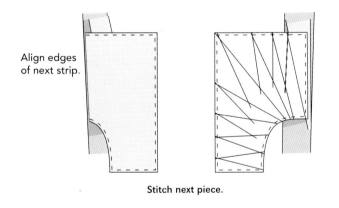

Align edges of next strip.

Stitch next piece.

7. Fold the fabric to the left, and trim the excess fabric at the top and bottom.

8. Continue this process until the arc is covered. You may want to lightly spray starch the fabric while it is still attached to the paper. This stabilizes the threads. Do not put the iron on the paper where the ink is, as the ink will come off on your iron. Trim the fabric along the outside lines of the paper pattern. Place a pin on the bottom curve where you see a black dot on the stitching line of each arc. This is a matching point for attaching Piece A. Tear off the paper. (Because you have scored the paper on each line before stitching, it will tear off easily.)

PUTTING TOGETHER THE PIECES

1. Make ⅛″ clips about every ¾″ on the inside curve of the pieced arc. This will open up the curve when you attach it to Piece A.

2. Choose a Piece A for the bottom of the arc, making sure you choose the correct color to match the points. Place a pin where you see a black dot on the stitching line on Piece A. Match up the black dots on the arc and Piece A, right sides together, and pin. Then go to each end of the arc and match up the side seams of the arc and Piece A, and pin through the fabrics.

3. Lengthen the machine stitch length to the normal setting. Pin as needed. Keeping the arc on top, stitch the pieces together using a ¼″ seam allowance. With the clipping, the seam will open up to fit Piece A. Press.

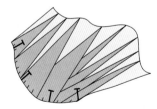

Pin A to pieced points.

4. Make 4 blocks with a dark background, bright points, and bright centers. Make 4 with a bright background, dark points, and dark centers. Set aside.

FILLER BLOCKS AND JOINING SECTIONS TOGETHER

Filler Sections

These sections are made with the 27 dark and medium-bright $1\frac{1}{2}'' \times 5\frac{1}{2}''$ pieces and the theme-print rectangles you have cut. All these rectangles have $5\frac{1}{2}''$ as a dimension, so only the other measurement is given. The narrow strips are always $1\frac{1}{2}'' \times 5\frac{1}{2}''$. Label each section.

1. Make A3 as shown.

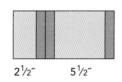

$2\frac{1}{2}''$ $5\frac{1}{2}''$

2. Make A4.

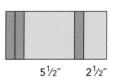

$5\frac{1}{2}''$ $2\frac{1}{2}''$

3. Make B2.

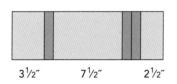

$3\frac{1}{2}''$ $7\frac{1}{2}''$ $2\frac{1}{2}''$

4. Make 1 for B3 and 1 for B5.

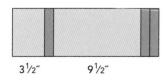

$3\frac{1}{2}''$ $9\frac{1}{2}''$

5. Make C1.

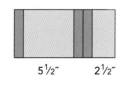

$5\frac{1}{2}''$ $2\frac{1}{2}''$

6. Make D2.

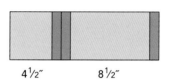

$2\frac{1}{2}''$ $7\frac{1}{2}''$ $3\frac{1}{2}''$

7. Make D4.

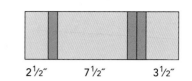

$4\frac{1}{2}''$ $8\frac{1}{2}''$

8. Make D5.

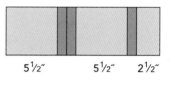

$5\frac{1}{2}''$ $5\frac{1}{2}''$ $2\frac{1}{2}''$

Sections

Refer to the Section Diagram, and arrange the filler blocks with the Firefly blocks as shown. Make Sections A–D. Be sure to press all the seams.

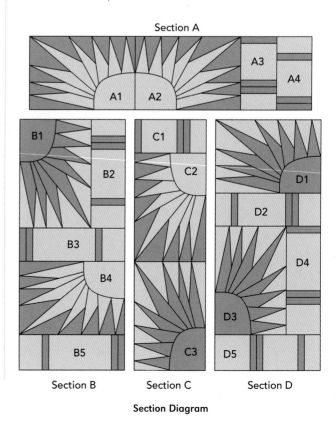

Section A

Section B   Section C   Section D

Section Diagram

MAKE THE QUILT

1. Refer to the Section Diagram to join the sections together. Join B to C, B/C to D, and then join A to the top of B/C/D.

2. Sew the 1½″ × 45½″ inner borders to the sides of the quilt top, and press. Add the 1½″ × 42½″ inner borders to the top and bottom of the quilt top, and press again.

3. Sew the 3″ × 47½″ outer borders to the sides of the quilt top, and press. Add the 3″ × 47½″ outer borders to the top and bottom of the quilt top, and press again.

FINISHING

1. Layer the backing, batting, and quilt top. Baste, and quilt as desired.

2. Bind using your preferred method.

Quilt Assembly Diagram

ECHO QUILTING

The large-scale print inspired the quilting in *Firefly*.
A curved shape from the print fills in the points of
the New York Beauty blocks, and part of a flower is
repeated in the centers of the blocks. The swirls in the
backgrounds of the New York Beauty blocks add movement to the quilt. The quilting around the dahlias
continues the design into the solid fabrics, creating
the feeling of flowers moving through the quilt.

Repeating the design of the print integrates the blocks
and the filler sections. Using your prints as inspiration
for quilting can be the best way to make your quilt
sing. You can simplify the designs, make them different
sizes, or use parts of the fabric to create the quilting
lines. Be inventive, and think of ways to create interesting
quilting from the designs in your prints.

Improving Your Paper-Foundation Piecing

1. If you need to tape together the paper to make it
large enough, just tape in the areas where you won't
be stitching.

2. For precision, make copies of the patterns using
a copier.

3. Use a piece of template plastic, and fold on the piecing
lines to make it easier to remove the paper after stitching.

4. Set the machine stitch length to 1.5, or 18 stitches to the
inch. This will make it easier to remove the paper.

5. You may want to lightly spray starch the fabric while it is
still attached to the paper. This stabilizes the threads.

6. Do not put the iron on the paper where the lines are
printed; they will come off on your iron.

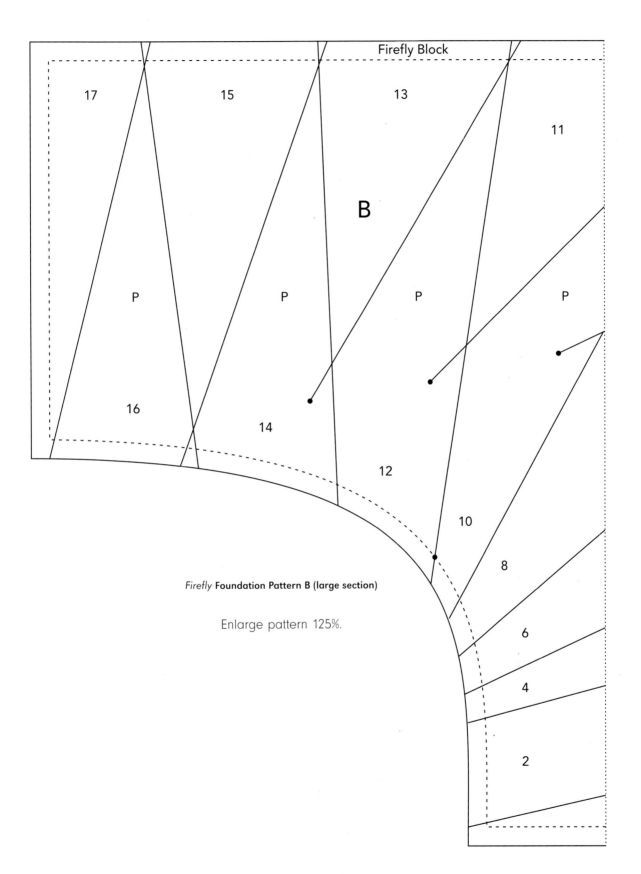

Firefly Block

17

15

13

11

B

P

P

P

P

16

14

12

10

8

6

4

2

Firefly **Foundation Pattern B (large section)**

Enlarge pattern 125%.

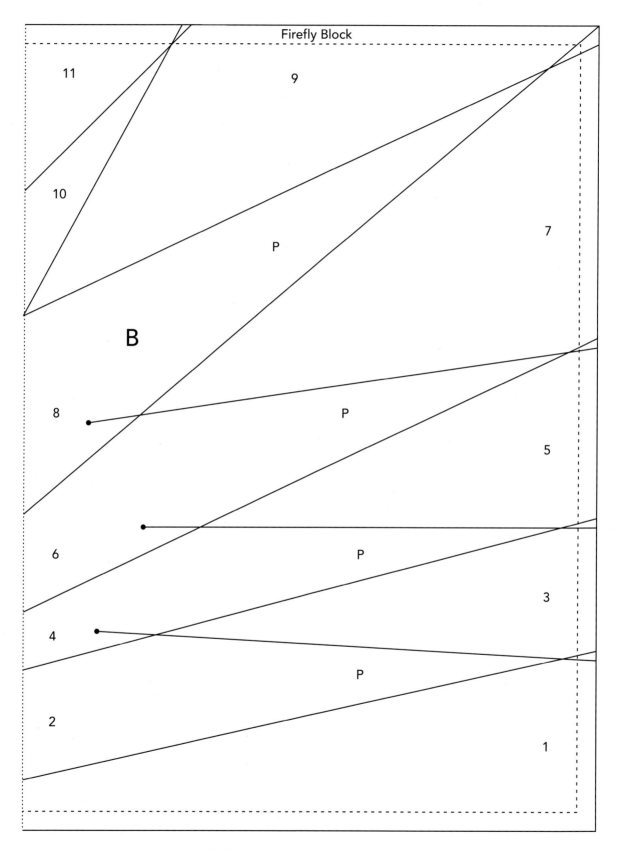

Firefly **Foundation Pattern B (small section)**

Enlarge pattern 125%.

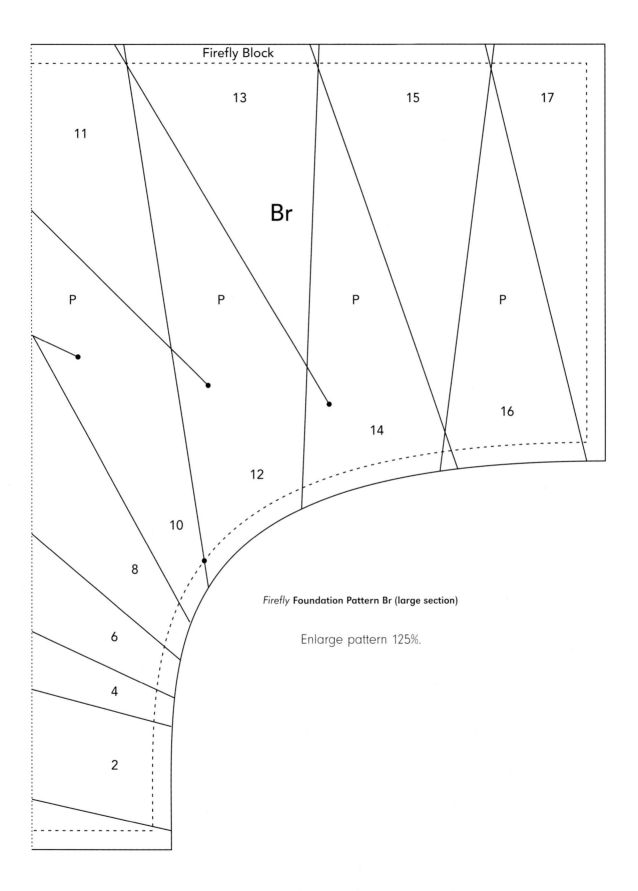

Firefly Block

Br

11

13

15

17

P

P

P

P

16

14

12

10

8

6

4

2

Firefly **Foundation Pattern Br (large section)**

Enlarge pattern 125%.

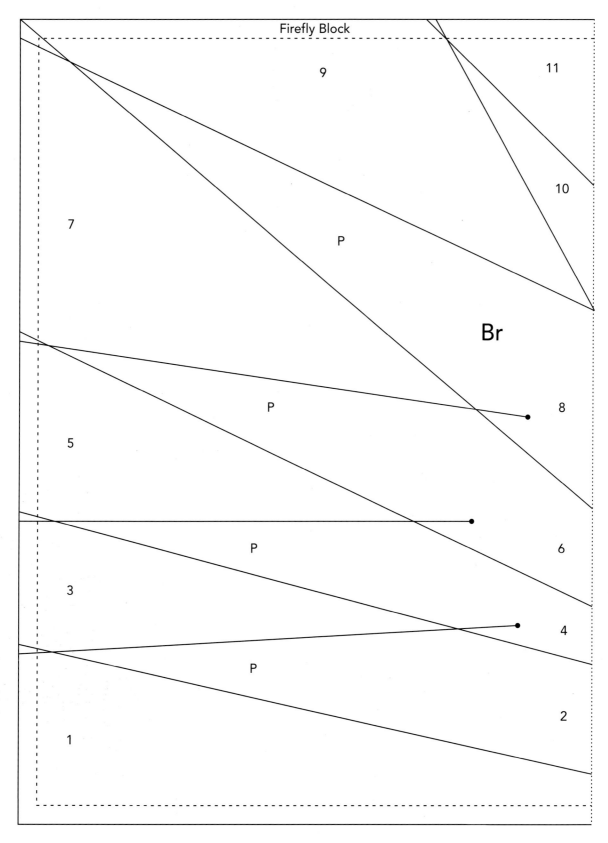

Firefly Block

9

11

10

7

P

Br

P

8

5

P

6

3

P

4

P

2

1

Firefly **Foundation Pattern Br (small section)**

Enlarge pattern 125%.

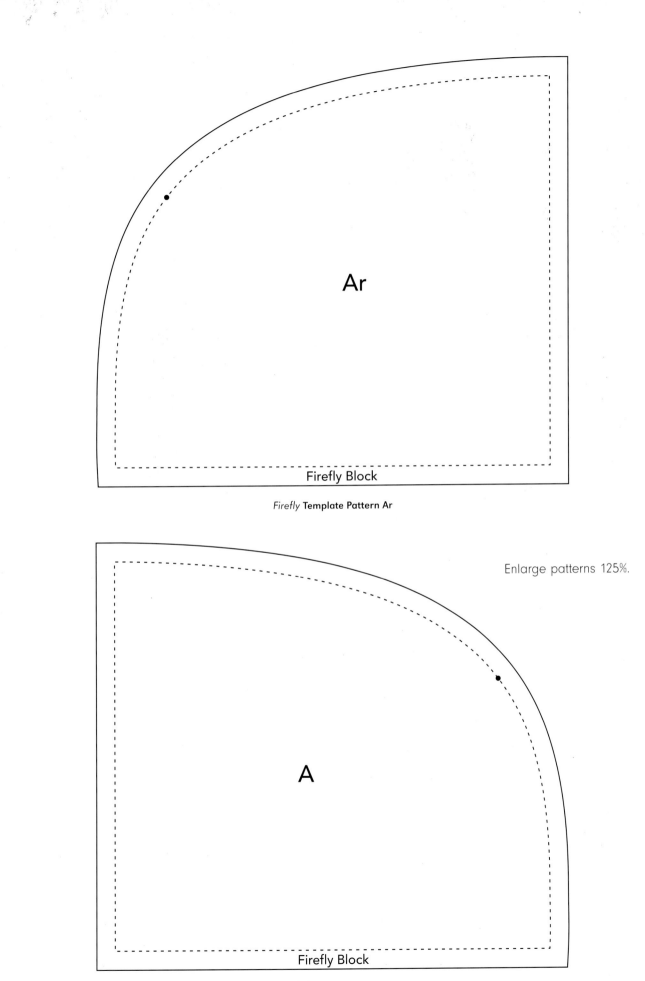

Ar

Firefly Block

Firefly **Template Pattern Ar**

Enlarge patterns 125%.

A

Firefly Block

Firefly **Template Pattern A**

LILY POND

Made by Jean Wells. Finished size: 40˝ × 29½˝

① **FABRIC:** Solid-like

② **PIECING:** Straight, paper piecing, and strip piecing

③ **QUILTING:** Fluid

Photographs of lilies in a pond gave me the idea of reducing the size of the block I used in *Firefly* (page 75) and piecing it in lily colors. Once the block was reduced, I drafted petals in the center portion to more accurately represent an actual water lily. Lily ponds are so serene and calming. Fabrics in green tones from blue-green to olive create this mood in the strip-pieced water.

Batiks are perfect for this quilt because of the slight color changes that you get when you cut across the width of the fabric. The strips look like light hitting the water. There are also contemporary landscape-style fabrics available that work well. If you paint fabric, you can create both lily and water fabric in colors and patterns that reflect your idea of serenity.

Once you have your fabrics, take a look at the tip on page 92 for a painterly way to use your palette of colors.

MATERIALS

- ¼ yard yellow for flowers
- ¼ yard peach or melon for flowers
- ⅓ yard light pink for flowers
- ⅓ yard medium pink for flowers
- ⅓ yard bright pink for flowers
- 2¼ yards total of greens for backgrounds and sashing
- 1 yard for backing
- ⅓ yard for binding
- 44″ × 34″ batting
- Foundation paper (see Resources on page 95)
- Monofilament or invisible thread (smoke color)
- 3″ × 5″ piece of template plastic
- Optional: Add-a-Quarter ruler for the flower petals

CUTTING

Yellow:

Cut 4 strips 1½″ × 42″ for the flower center background.

Melon and pinks:

Cut 4 strips 1¼″ × 42″, one from each of the flower fabrics, for the flower center points.

Cut 11 strips 2½″ × 42″ from the flower fabrics for the flower petals. Use a variety of shades.

Greens:

Cut 11 strips 3¾″ × 42″ for the background of the water lilies.

Cut 1 strip 2″ × 42″ for the top of the quilt.

Cut 8 strips 1¼″ × 42″ for the sashing. Use a variety of shades.

Cut 4 strips 1″ × 42″ for the sashing. Use a variety of shades.

Cut 2 strips ¾″ × 42″ for the strips between the blocks. Use a variety of shades.

Cut 8 strips 1″ × 42″ for the strips between the blocks. Use a variety of shades.

Cut 2 strips 1¼″ × 42″ for the strips between the blocks. Use a variety of shades.

Cut 4 strips 1½″ × 42″ for the strips between the blocks. Use a variety of shades.

ASSEMBLY

FLOWERS

1. Using foundation paper, make 7 copies of each Lily Pond pattern piece on pages 92–94. This is easiest to do on a copy machine.

2. Follow the paper-foundation piecing instructions for *Firefly* (pages 78–79) to construct the Lily Pond block sections.

My cues for color came from pictures of water lilies. Take a close look at the photograph. Some of the flowers are more melon or orange in color and some are more pink. The yellow is used in the background area of the center block. Mix up the colors as you make the flowers. See Using Painterly Piecing on page 92 for one way to mix up your colors.

3. Stitch together the right and left sides of each lily. Press.

4. On the pieced flower center, stitch around the top edge, $3/16$″ from the edge. Turn under the edge to the wrong side, and press. Place the flower center on top of the right and left sections, and pin in place. Either hand stitch the flower center to the flower or follow the instructions on page 52 for blind-hem-stitch appliqué. The Lily Pond block should measure $15\frac{1}{2}$″ × $5\frac{1}{2}$″.

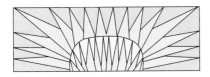

WATER

1. Use an accurate $\frac{1}{4}$″ seam, and stitch a 1″ green strip between two $1\frac{1}{4}$″ green strips. Press the seams in one direction. The strip set should measure $2\frac{1}{2}$″ wide. Repeat to make a total of 4 sashing strip sets. Set these aside.

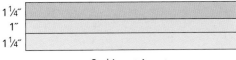

Sashing strip set

Make 4 sashing strip sets (measurements are cut widths).

2. Stitch 2 sets of strips together as shown for the water blocks between the flower blocks. The measurements are given for the cut green strips. Press the seams in one direction. Use an accurate $\frac{1}{4}$″ seam; the finished strip sets should measure $5\frac{1}{2}$″ wide.

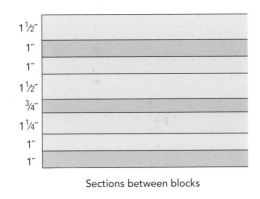

Sections between blocks

Make 2 strip sets for water blocks (measurements are cut widths).

3. Refer to the Quilt Assembly Diagram to identify each row as you cut sections from the pieced strips to insert. Arrange the Lily Pond blocks with these sections row by row on a design wall. Always keep the seams running horizontally.

Row 1: Cut 2 sections $5\frac{1}{2}$″ × $5\frac{1}{2}$″.

Row 2: Cut 1 section 7″ × $5\frac{1}{2}$″ and 1 section 4″ × $5\frac{1}{2}$″.

Row 3: Cut 2 sections $5\frac{1}{2}$″ × $5\frac{1}{2}$″.

Row 4: Cut 1 section $13\frac{1}{2}$″ × $5\frac{1}{2}$″ and 1 section $12\frac{1}{2}$″ × $5\frac{1}{2}$″.

4. Stitch each row together. Press.

5. On a design wall or a flat surface, arrange the rows, and place the sashing strips between the rows. Trim the sashing strips as needed to $40\frac{1}{2}$″.

6. Place the 2″ green strip at the top of the quilt. Trim the strip as needed.

7. Sew the sashing strips between the flower block rows. Sew the 2″ strip to the top. Press.

FINISHING

1. Layer the backing, batting, and quilt top. Baste, and quilt as desired or use the quilting suggestion below.

2. Bind using your preferred method.

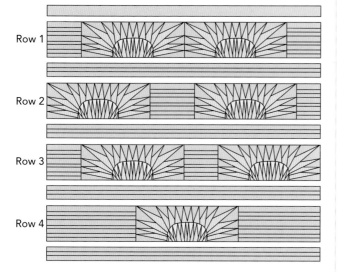

Quilt Assembly Diagram

FLUID QUILTING

Free-motion quilting provides the fluid, painterly look of brushstrokes for the petals of the lilies, and the suggestion of lily pads in the green water. By using threads that blend with the fabrics, you create quilting that is subtle and simple and that enhances the design instead of competing with it.

tips & techniques

Using Painterly Piecing

Here's a technique to use to achieve a random, painterly look in your piecing.

1. Cut the strips for the strip piecing.

2. Toss the strips into piles. For *Lily Pond*, you'll have one pile for the top of the block, with the green 3¾″-wide strips and the 2½″-wide flower strips, and one pile for the centers, with the 1½″-wide yellow and 1¼″-wide flower-color strips.

3. Randomly pick up strips as you piece. After you use part of a strip, toss what's left back into the pile.

4. Stand back and admire your artwork.

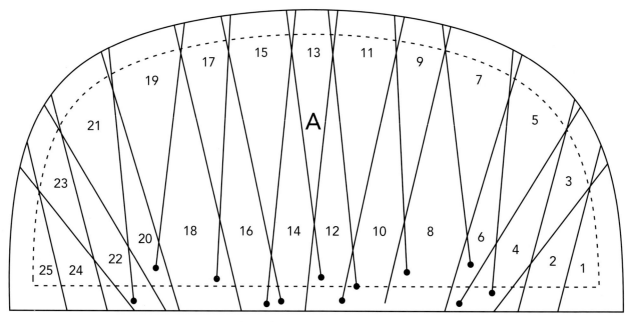

Lily Pond **Foundation Pattern Center**

Copy at 100%.

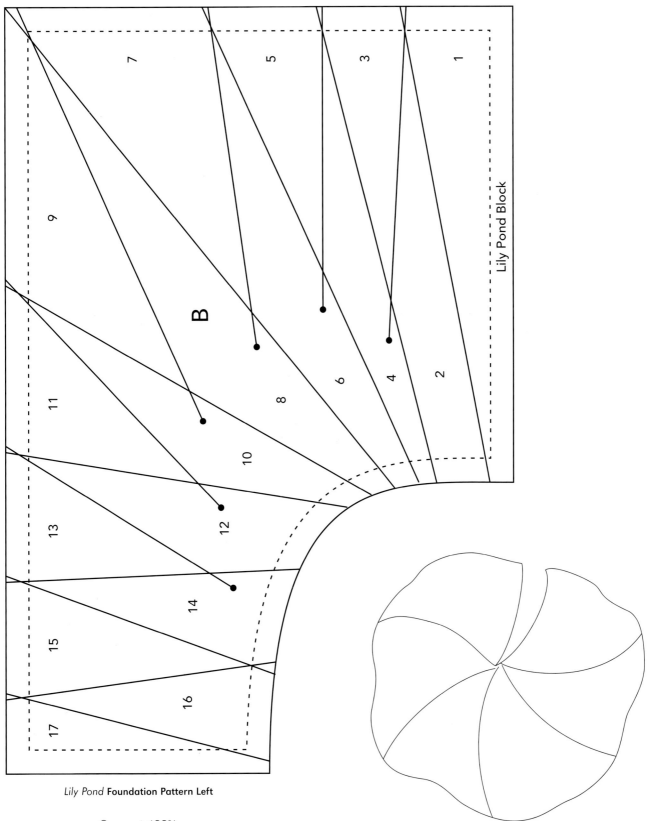

7

5

3

1

9

Lily Pond Block

B

6

4

2

8

11

10

13

12

15

14

16

17

Lily Pond **Foundation Pattern Left**

Copy at 100%.

Quilting: Use for inspiration or enlarge as desired.

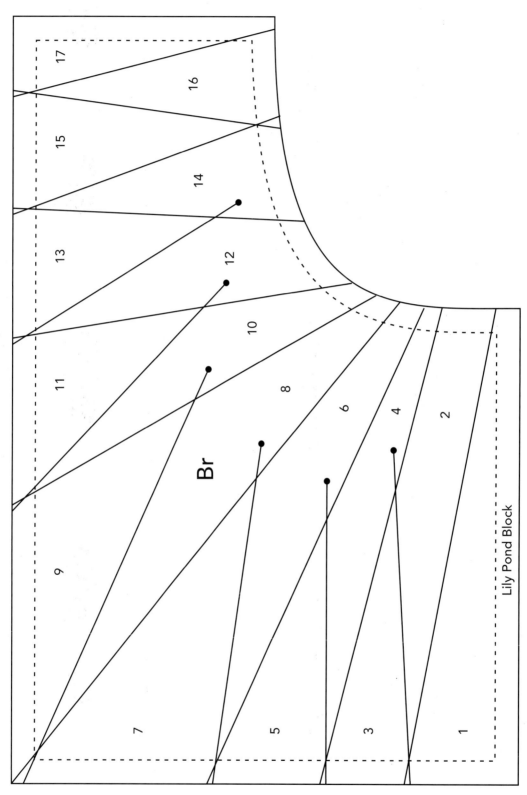

Lily Pond **Foundation Pattern Right**

Copy at 100%.

ABOUT THE AUTHOR

Valori Wells is a professional quilter, fabric designer, author, and pattern designer. Nine years ago, Valori joined The Stitchin' Post staff as notion, book, and pattern buyer. She is now the co-owner of the store with her mother, Jean Wells. Together they pool their ideas to keep the store on the cutting edge of quilting. Valori is also responsible for creating the store's website and managing The Quilter's Affair conference.

Valori has a bachelor's degree in fine arts, specializing in black-and-white photography. This background has contributed to her career as a fabric designer; her fabrics often portray larger-than-life flowers in updated palettes that appeal to the younger generation of quilters as well as the general quilting public. As a quilter, she is always designing quilts in her mind as she paints her fabric designs.

Valori lives in Sisters, Oregon, with her husband, Ross, and daughter, Olivia.

Other books by Valori Wells   **Books by Jean and Valori Wells**

RESOURCES

FOR PAPER-FOUNDATION PIECING

Carol Doak's Foundation Paper or Simple Foundations Vellum Paper

Find these at your local quilt shop or order from C&T Publishing.

FOR MORE INFORMATION

Ask for a free catalog:
C&T Publishing, Inc.
PO Box 1456
Lafayette, CA 94549
800-284-1114
email: ctinfo@ctpub.com
website: www.ctpub.com

QUILTING SUPPLIES

The Stitchin' Post
PO Box 280
311 W. Cascade
Sisters, OR 97759
541-549-6061
website: www.stitchinpost.com

Cotton Patch Mail Order
3404 Hall Lane
Dept. CTB
Lafayette, CA 94549
800-835-4418; 925-283-7883
email: CottonPa@aol.com
website: www.quiltusa.com

Note: Fabrics used in the quilts shown may not be currently available; fabric manufacturers keep most fabrics in print for only a short time.

C&T Publishing's professional photography services are now available to the public. Visit us at www.ctmediaservices.com.